FUNDAMENTALISM TODAY
What Makes It So Attractive?

To
my lumberjack
Tom

FUNDAMENTALISM TODAY
What Makes It So Attractive!

Edited by
Marla J. Selvidge

BRETHREN PRESS
Elgin, Illinois

FUNDAMENTALISM TODAY: What Makes It So Attractive?

Brethren Press, 1451 Dundee Avenue, Elgin, IL 60120

Cover design by VISTA III

Edited by Leslie R. Keylock

Scripture quotations are from the Revised Standard Version of the Bible, copyrighted 1946, 1952 © 1971, 1973 by the Division of Education and Ministry of the National Council of the Churches of Christ in the U.S.A. and are used by permission.

Library of Congress Cataloging in Publication Data

Main entry under title:

Fundamentalism today.

    1. Fundamentalism—Addresses, essays, lectures.
I. Selvidge, Marla J., 1948-
BT82.2.F84   1984   280'.4   84-16952
ISBN 0-87178-297-9

Printed in the United States of America

CONTENTS

FOREWORD

Jerry Falwell

In recent years there has been renewed interest in Protestant fundamentalism. The news media, as well as mainline Protestant clergymen and professors, have analyzed and critiqued this conservative branch of Christianity to an unusual degree. I believe this attention has come about for several reasons: the comparative success of fundamentalists at building aggressive, growing churches, utilizing the mediums of television and radio to present the gospel, and our entrance into political activism. At least the subjects discussed in this book create that impression.

One has to believe that writers in general, and the authors of this book in particular, are sincere in their efforts and desire to address what they consider to be weaknesses in fundamentalism. Yet while these critics try to be objective and seem to understand us relatively well, they still improperly represent some of our characteristics. Occasionally, the writers' biases and prejudices get in the way of fair analysis. Nevertheless, fundamentalists must be aware of how we are perceived by others.

Scores of books have been written on fundamentalism and the New Right. Unfortunately, very few authors have personally interviewed fundamentalist leaders or traveled to do on-site research of our movement and its institutions. Too much of the published material has been written from "ivory towers" and is therefore somewhat uninformed and distorted. Parts of this book reveal that. I must say that I feel the news media have examined fundamentalism more thoroughly even though not always fairly.

Fundamentalism is becoming increasingly difficult to stereotype, having two basic contingents. One is the classic unbending militant group. The other is younger and more thoughtful. The former will have a defensive reaction to this book and ignore the critique. But mainliners usually ignore our indictments too. On the other hand, the latter will agree with some issues presented—to a certain extent some of the reservations and questions raised here have already been expressed.

I am executive editor of *Fundamentalist Journal*. Ironically, Edward Dobson, in his monthly "Fundamentalism Today" column, has dared to consistently confront fundamentalism with our own weaknesses. The response to his editorials has made us keenly aware that some fundamentalists strongly oppose our suggesting there are methodologies or sensitive traditions that may need to be examined and changed. Fundamentalists find it hard to admit that we may be wrong or need to change. But sometimes we *are* wrong and sometimes we *do* need to change. Even so, I believe that mainline churches can also learn from us.

There will always be disagreement and tension between fundamentalism and mainline Protestantism. I think it is necessary for all of us.

INTRODUCTION

Marla J. Selvidge

Fundamentalism Today: What Makes It So Attractive? is a collection of thoughts by a variety of people from both Protestant and Catholic religious backgrounds. They have experienced or discovered fundamentalist thinking and fundamentalist theology. Some defend it, others gently criticize it for its narrowness. Their thoughts are important because together they make a statement. People can hold differing opinions, even opposing opinions, and still talk to each other. They can look at a very volatile issue and discover that each person has something to contribute. For instance, Vince Branick celebrates, in principle, the literal interpretation of the Bible. He thinks it is a more serious approach than the historical-critical method.

Many of the writers take a hard, critical look at fundamentalism. Whether in history (Rausch), in print (Collins), on television (Zukowski), in science classrooms (Moore and Barnes), in the exercise of faith (Shinn) or bibliolatry (Towne), fundamentalism needs to be discussed. It is a vital force in our political system (Pierard) and can be abused by those in power. According to Peggy Shriver, who imagines herself standing in the shoes of a fundamentalist, life is not so easy these days. The world that the fundamentalist is inheriting also belongs to the liberal. Tyron Inbody sounds an alarm to the liberals. They may find themselves in a similar situation as the fundamentalists soon. The threat of nuclear holocaust is a very real terror for everyone.

* * * * * * * * * * * * * * *

Many thanks to all of the graduate assistants in the religious studies department at the University of Dayton during 1983-1984. They were a constant source of support to me. John Riedeman deserves a round of applause for typing the manuscript and working through the editing task with me in the summer of 1984.

1
FUNDAMENTALIST ORIGINS

David Rausch

In Oberlin a husband and wife were accused of starving to death their little girl because little girls are not as "important" as little boys. The newswoman announced to all of Northern Ohio, *"They* are Christian fundamentalists!"

A couple in Tennessee who believe in faith healing refused to let their child undergo medical treatment and were forced by the court to let such treatment commence. The newsman insisted, "They are fundamentalists!"

Are these stories typical of fundamentalists? Just what is a fundamentalist?

Part of the problem with the word "fundamentalism" is one of definition. For example, Ayatollah Khomeini and his followers in Iran are known in some circles as Islamic or Muslim "fundamentalists." If this association is made on the American scene, it certainly does not leave people with a positive attitude toward American fundamentalists. If every right-wing fanatic or schismatic is a "fundamentalist," we have irreparably muddied the waters of scholarly analysis concerning this religious movement and phenomenon. We will have defeated our intellectual pursuit before we begin.

For this reason it is important to examine the origins of fundamentalism. We must carefully investigate the roots of American fundamentalism and the early usage of the term if we are going to get a historical perspective on this modern religious movement.

The term "fundamentals" emerged at the turn of this century. In fact, one of the main compilations of the early fundamentalist movement was *The Fundamentals,* a series of twelve volumes published between 1910 and 1915 to reaffirm the "fundamentals" of Christianity. Early fundamentalist opinion covering a wide range of doctrinal issues is delineated in these volumes (sixty-four different authors wrote ninety articles). The virgin birth, the deity of Christ, his vicarious death, his resurrection, the Holy Spirit, missions, evangelism, other religions, and even personal testimonies are included. Nearly thirty of the articles defend the verbal inspiration of the Bible. An impressive group of conservative scholars from latter-nineteenth-century evangelicalism wrote many of the articles. They include B. B. Warfield of Princeton Theological Seminary; Melvin Kyle of Xenia Seminary; George Frederick Wright, professor of geology at Oberlin College; George L. Robinson, an archeologist at McCormick Seminary in Chicago; and James Orr, professor of theology at the United Free Church College in Glasgow, Scotland. Each of them had an established reputation for scholarship.

Over three million copies of *The Fundamentals* were published. Hence, the term "fundamentals" was in use at the turn of this century. Most assuredly the phrase "a return to the fundamentals" of the Christian faith was commonly used in evangelical churches. In 1919 the World's Christian Fundamentals Association was founded at a Bible conference in Philadelphia, instigated by several leaders of the early fundamentalist movement. In July 1920 Curtis Lee Laws, editor of the Baptist *Watchman-Examiner*, used the word "fundamentalist" in an editorial. In 1922 Harry Emerson Fosdick, a professor at Union Theological Seminary in New York and a pastor, wrote and preached his famous sermon "Shall the Fundamentalists Win?" He was determined they would not.

In the nineteenth century most mainline Protestant churches considered themselves "evangelical." A century ago Episcopalians, Methodists, Presbyterians, and Baptists were all within the framework of evangelicalism. Their eschatology was *post*millennial. In other words, they believed that the Protestant Christian church would bring in the millennium, the thousand year period of peace spoken of in the book of Revelation. The Protestant Christian church would "Christianize" the world. It would become progressively better, and *then* Jesus Christ would return. This was the great century for Christian missionary societies, the goal of which was not only to evangelize but to "remake" American society—in fact to "remake" the world.

Historians have caricatured this phenomenon as "the Benevolent Empire." The religious belief in the United States as a Christian, i.e., Protestant, nation and the *"New* Israel" had an impact on the nation's involvement in foreign affairs, its attitudes toward immigrants, and imperialism throughout the nineteenth century. It created a civil religion that permeated the nation. Postmillennial evangelicalism was the "in" religion. It was socially acceptable and dominated the culture of the nineteenth century. Even the Civil War could not daunt the optimism of postmillennialism. It was not until World War I that Protestant postmillennialism suffered a stunning setback. Today there are very few postmillennial theologians.

Two significant theological changes sprouted during the nineteenth century. The resultant debate took place *within* evangelicalism. The staunchest supporters on *both* sides were evangelicals. And what were these two critical theological changes of the latter nineteenth century? They were the "higher criticism" of the Bible and Darwin's theory of evolution as applied not only to the origins of humanity but to the evolution of religion itself. Thus, a conflict in nineteenth-century evangelicalism emerged. Postmillennial evangelical scholars such as the Princeton theologians Charles Hodge and B. B. Warfield defended the conservative side. The liberal evangelical view was championed by scholars like Walter Rauschenbusch and William Newton Clarke.

The debate became intense as theological views began to change in the nineteenth century. For example, in April 1899 at a New York meeting of *evangelical* Methodist pastors Dr. S. P. Cadman declared, "The absolute inerrancy and infallibility of the Bible are no longer possible of belief among reasoning men. . . . Half the pages of the Old Testament are of unknown authorship, and the New Testament contains contradictions." Several hundred *evangelical* Methodist ministers applauded his remarks. Arno C. Gaebelein, a Methodist who later became a leader in the fundamentalist-evangelical movement, was horrified. He asked high officials to bring charges against any evangelical who would attack the Bible in this manner. The "high officials" suggested that he should "not be hasty" for "sooner or later we must fall in line with the results of scholarly biblical criticism."

The fundamentalist movement arose in this atmosphere of intellectual and theological debate between conservatives and liberals within the evangelical intelligentsia of the northern

United States. Notice that it is *not* a redneck, rural, Southern, agrarian phenomenon. It occurred in the mainline churches among leaders with earned doctorates, and in major urban areas.

The fundamentalist evangelicals, in fact, hold to nineteenth-century conservative evangelical theology—with one important difference. They had a *"premillennial"* eschatology. They believed Christ would return *before* the start of the thousand-year period of peace. In this perspective the United States is not a Christian nation, nor is the church the new Israel. Premillenarians believed that the world was going to get *worse*. Only Jesus Christ would be able to pull things together and personally institute the millennium.

Most liberal theologians were horrified at premillennial eschatology. A good example is an article by Shirley Jackson Case, professor of early church history and New Testament interpretation at the University of Chicago. It was published in the respected scholarly journal *The Biblical World* in July 1918. At that time the U.S. had become involved in World War I. Case attempts to use the war "hysteria" to attack premillennial doctrine. He labels it "anti-War," "pacifist," and "socialistic." This is ironic. Fundamentalists soon after became known as avid "Communist fighters" because they believed the Bible said Russia (the "king of the North") would once again become a great evil power. Their belief in the rise of the anti-Christ and intense evil in the world alerted them to the dangers of Communism (much as Aleksandr Solzhenitsyn has alerted us) and even to believe the reality of the Jewish Holocaust under the Nazi regime at a time when more liberal Christians considered such accounts "atrocity propaganda."

Case's intense hatred of premillennialism and his ad hominem arguments are indicative of the age. He wrote:

> The American nation is engaged in a gigantic effort to make the world safe for democracy. While pledged to give unreservedly of its blood and treasure for the attainment of this ideal, there are those in our midst who declare that the undertaking is foredoomed to failure. The writer has before him a recent letter containing these oracular words: "If it were not pathetic it would be silly to think that democracy, if it prevails, will cause wars to cease. The men

who believe this are simply chasing a phantom that will always elude them. There is no solution except the coming of Christ as he foretold." . . . Under ordinary circumstances one might excusably pass over premillenarianism as a wild and relatively harmless fancy. But in the present time of testing it would be almost traitorous negligence to ignore the detrimental character of the premillennial propaganda. By proclaiming that wars cannot be eliminated until Christ returns and that in the meantime the world must grow constantly worse, this type of teaching strikes at the very root of our present national endeavor to bring about a new day for humanity, when this old earth shall be made a better place in which to live, and a new democracy shall arise to render wars impossible.

"At the present moment," asserted Case, "premillenarianism is a serious menace to our democracy and is all the more dangerous because it masquerades under the cloak of piety."

Case later suggested that "the premillennialist might well want Germany to win," and alluded to the fact that "enemy gold" might be financing their movement.

> The principles of premillennialism readily lend themselves to the purpose of the I.W.W. [International Workers of the World—the socialist trade union] propaganda, with its radical hatred of all organized society and its vigorous antiwar polemic.

In addition, Case's diatribe is a subtle insight into the spread of the movement. He complained:

> There is something very suggestive about the extent and vigor of premillennial activities in recent times. If these activities were confined to a few obscure sects the danger might be comparatively insignificant, but this virus has been injected into the spiritual veins of large numbers of people in various denominations. A prominent eastern minister in one of the larger Protestant bodies painfully confesses that his denomination "is cracked from sea to sea," some of its most influential pulpits even being occupied by men who are actively indoctrinating their audiences into this vicious teaching. Already the menace has

assumed such proportions that Christian leaders among Methodists, Baptists, Presbyterians, and similarly influential bodies are beginning to realize the necessity of actively opposing the pernicious propaganda.

Near the end of his article Case sounded more like a modern fundamentalist than a liberal theologian. He emphasized, "Concretely our special task is that of defending the sacred rights of democracy and helping to make this ideal supreme in all international relationships."

One could draw many interesting points from Case's article as well as from other articles of the period. The central point, however, is that *premillennialism* and the *verbal inspiration* of the Bible are definitive characteristics of the early fundamentalist movement—characteristics recognized by its opponents as well as its advocates. The character of the fundamentalist movement was determined long before the Scopes Trial in 1925. The battle lines were clearly drawn and maintained by liberal as well as conservative theologicans—liberal theologians who on many other topics were broad and flexible. On the other hand, this early fundamentalist movement was *militant* toward what it considered "doctrinal apostasy" (evolutionary theory and critical methods that its members felt sought to discredit the Bible). Premillennial fundamentalists worked hand in hand with postmillennial conservative evangelicals to battle such "apostasy."

Conservative alliances are not unique to our present day. Warfield, Wright, and Robinson, though postmillennialists, appear in *The Fundamentals.* A conservative theological alliance had been formed. However, postmillennial writers were not given essays on the future or on prophecy. That particular area was reserved for premillenarians such as Arno C. Gaebelein. Right or wrong, premillennial fundamentalists did not feel they were pessimistic about world conditions. They felt they were realistic. Fundamentalists believed that the Bible outlined the future of the world. Accordingly they set out to conform their attitudes and actions to their view of the Bible. Many of the characteristics of the contemporary fundamentalist movement were molded during this early period.

The movement maintained a conservative lifestyle. This

lifestyle was not really outside of the culture. In the 1920s the U.S.A. voted in prohibition. Mainline denominations, including the Federal Council of Churches, supported it. Early fundamentalists emphasized missions and evangelism. They believed strongly in education, although they feared current educational philosophy. They stressed the written and spoken word. They employed tracts, publications, and periodicals, and encouraged Bible study in Bible and prophecy conferences, Bible institutes, and Bible colleges. Many of these have survived to become Christian liberal arts colleges. Fundamentalists opposed Pentecostalism and the sanctification teaching of some of the holiness churches. Pentecostalism in general adopted fundamentalist theology, except on spiritual gifts, including in many cases premillennial eschatology, as would many of the holiness churches. It is, nevertheless, inaccurate to include these separate religious movements in fundamentalism. This is also true of the charismatic movement today. (The black church also should not be included in fundamentalism, although there are definite theological links at times.)

Fundamentalism was pro-Jewish, pro-Zionist and pro-Israel (based on its eschatology), but it continued the nativist anti-Catholic stance of Protestantism in the nineteenth century. One finds definite antiabortion and profamily stances in the early movement as well as negative attitudes toward women in the pulpit ministry. Members persistently battled what they believed was America's plunge into immorality.

During the 1920s, 1930s, and 1940s a militant fundamentalism emerged—a separatistic movement much more volatile than the intellectually based fundamentalism of the latter nineteenth century. Adherents of this militant faction seized the name "fundamentalist" and used it as a battle cry. The fundamentalist evangelicals in mainline churches and other denominations watched the media as they publicized this development. The word "fundamentalist" began to acquire an unfavorable connotation. More moderate individuals who did not want to be associated with the newly assumed connotation of the word fundamentalist began to call themselves evangelicals by the 1940s. The term seemed appropriate. The nation was no longer evangelical as a result of massive immigration at the turn of the century. Religion itself was dominated by those

proud to be called "liberals." To more moderate fundamentalists "evangelical" now meant something. Some even suggested
that they adopt the term "neoevangelical." I call them fundamentalist evangelicals. For example, Billy Graham is part of the
historic fundamentalist-evangelical trend flowing from the
nineteenth century to the present. Jerry Falwell would be part
of separatistic fundamentalism, the smaller right wing of fundamentalist evangelicalism. They were a relatively small group
that grew in the 1960s and 1970s through "superchurches."

Both groups are basically premillennial, although the
fundamentalist evangelical is lost in the broad sea that the term
"evangelical" now describes. Today the term "evangelical" and
its effectiveness as a label is being debated in a society in which
a large percentage of the population claims to be "born again."

In the past few years the spectre of political fundamentalism has been in the news. Jerry Falwell and the Moral Majority
have caused quite a furor. It is ironic that such a furor is being
raised over political fundamentalism because a decade ago
fundamentalists were charged with being "apolitical." They
were accused of not using the political process in the moral
causes of civil rights, poverty, and peace. In fact, they were
criticized for shunning the political process altogether. Jerry
Falwell had stated in the 1960s (as some fundamentalists still do)
that the Christian was not to be involved in politics and political
lobbying. In a 1965 sermon entitled "Ministers and Marches"
he declared, "Nowhere are we commissioned to reform the
externals [of society]." The closest that the fundamentalist
movement had come to overt political activity was their
vociferous support of Israel and its right to exist. In other ways,
however, fundamentalist evangelicals had kept up with politics
and had strident viewpoints. A perusal of fundamentalist evangelical periodicals during the 1930s would certainly bear out
their concern during the upheaval of the Depression. In addition, their anti-Communist stance was a foray into the political
system. But nothing on the lines of the Moral Majority lobby
was advocated.

What we viewed in the 1970s was in some ways analagous
to what happened in the nineteenth century. Falwell and others
felt that a crucial part of American life was slipping away from
the American people. The Supreme Court decisions, especially

the decision on abortion, were the turning point for Falwell personally. A coalition was formed, but not a theological one—rather, a *political* one. A conservative lobby was conceived that included Catholics and Jews. Falwell insists that he is not trying to create a "Christian" nation. This would be against his eschatology, which is very important to him. He claims that he does not oppose pluralism, but vows to protect the "absolute freedom to preach whatever religious conviction one might have, without ever impinging on the liberties and freedom of others." And yet, present in every political alliance are grave dangers, dangers of which fundamentalists such as Falwell must be keenly aware. There are radical groups on the horizon, even racist groups, that are attempting to influence fundamentalists for their own ends. There are extreme biblical literalists who maintain agendas potentially capable of depriving Americans of their own freedoms.

Those acquainted with *The Christian Century* know of my personal concern about the Christian Reconstructionist movement or Theonomists. This postmillennial movement does seek a "Christian nation" and lacks a respect for pluralism. It is trying to use political fundamentalism for its own ends. I believe they should be ethically opposed.

In another vein, conspiracy theory is currently debilitating the lives of naive Christian people and drawing them into a web of hatred that for many is inescapable.

I believe we have to face these problems. I note Falwell and the Moral Majority lobby as an example because we have frequently heard of their supposed political "influence," an influence I am not convinced exists.

Jerry Falwell, as well as other writers, would deemphasize premillennial eschatology as a basic characteristic of fundamentalism. And yet, in my estimation, it is definitely the historic key to the movement. This key guides Falwell's own political attitudes. Falwell himself in the pattern of the militant fundamentalism of the 1920s, 1930s, and 1940s asserts that *lifestyle* and *separation* are the keys to the movement. He declares in his book *The Fundamentalist Phenomenon* that "one may choose among premillennial, postmillennial, amillennial, pretribulational, midtribulational, posttribulational, partial rapture, and other views." However, I find it quite interesting that in a footnote Falwell states, "On the issues related to the doctrine of the Second Coming, see the national best seller by Hal Lindsay, *The Late Great Planet Earth* . . . ." Three other premillennial authors are also listed, including John Walvoord, the president of Dallas Theological Seminary. Why Hal Lindsay's book? In spite of his flexible comment Jerry Falwell did not allow a footnote advocating a postmillennial or amillennial position to lead his flock astray! From prophecy to politics some emphases may have been changed, but fundamentalist origins are grounded and visible today in premillennial eschatology.

2

THE ATTRACTIVENESS
OF FUNDAMENTALISM

Vincent P. Branick

"Are you trying to tell us that Jesus really didn't give the Sermon on the Mount?"

"How can you say that the Gospel of Matthew wasn't written by the apostle?"

These are students who often begin my New Testament class with a certain light in their eyes. They came to hear the Word of God.

They found instead the Two-Source Theory and biblical criticism.

At moments like these I envy the fundamentalist approach to the Bible. At moments like these I can sense the intense attractiveness of fundamentalism and thus the challenge to any practitioner of the historical-critical method. I want to reflect on some general issues of biblical interpretation, fundamentalist shortcuts, and aspects of understanding that touch the most basic philosophical presuppositions of knowledge.

James Barr in his critique of fundamentalism correctly points to the heart of the fundamentalist approach to Scripture. It lies not in a blind literalism. On the contrary, modern fundamentalist writers are speedy to forego a literal interpretation for the most bizarre symbolic or figurative reading whenever the truth of the Bible is at stake. It is this emphasis on the inerrancy or truth of Scripture that constitutes the heart of the fundamentalist approach as well as its most attractive feature. Fundamentalists see this biblical truth as referential truth, a correspondence between the details of the text and some event or reality outside the text. By so doing they assure the doubly attractive features of "seriousness" and "coherence" in Bible interpretation.

Seriousness and Coherence

Historical criticism as *critical* has long insisted on an objective reading of Scripture. The historical critic, furthermore, models this objectivity on that of the empirical sciences, where a personal distancing from the object, a certain neutrality before the proposed discovery, forms a necessary presupposition to correct procedure. Absolute neutrality is impossible, but the empirical method requires enough detachment to allow questions to be asked and to let the data speak for themselves. For objective results people don't want a tobacco company to research the relationship between smoking and lung cancer. In somewhat the same way historical critics do not set out to "prove" that the Bible is right. They want to know what an author or some community meant when it produced a particular piece of literature. Critical scholars intend to let the text speak regardless of how they might want it to speak.

In so doing historical criticism must bracket the truth question. It does not question whether the text accurately describes the way things are or were concerning God and humanity. It asks, rather, how the text relates to the linguistic constraints and possiblities arising from the authors' world. It deals with "meaning" or "nonsense," not "truth" or "error." As Barr insists, "The critical approach to biblical literature is the one in which it becomes (for the first time!) possible to understand the literature without having to use the category 'error'."

Some might find in this approach a cause to celebrate. The method certainly avoids the manipulations of Scripture and the sectarianism that characterizes much of the history of biblical interpretation.

Yet in another way this approach lacks a certain seriousness. At times it smacks of the playfulness of a game. A game may, of course, involve exhausting activity and energy and within its own context elicit intense seriousness. Yet a game can be put aside at will. A game is bounded off from the whole of life without direct claim on outside areas. It may suggest or represent the whole in microcosm. That is what makes it absorbing. But a game does not engage the whole. That is what makes it fun. To the degree that the historical-critical method requires that I distance myself and my life decisions from the matter at hand, to the degree the method renders me a detached observer of the Bible "out there," it becomes a game. Such playfulness fails to do justice to the subject matter of Scripture.

Let me illustrate. A student once asked me to state my position on a delicate issue. I attempted to do so with care and precision. After an arduous effort, I looked for a response. My questioner answered simply, "Well, now I know where you stand." I felt insulted. The questioner had played a game with me. I was simply performing for him. He did not allow *what* I said to summon him to some reaction. I wanted him to accept or reject what I had to say. I wanted the potential truth of my statements to exercise its power on him. Instead he was interested only in my position.

Likewise from the perspective of historical criticism the text does not speak to us. It speaks to its own audience in a distant historical context. We are separated today from that historical situation by all the cultural and chronological gaps that separate one historical context from another. The idea of attempting to read Scripture suggests the image of a fish in one fish bowl trying to listen to another fish in another fish bowl.

Very similar issues arise in "popular" programs for reading the classics of Western civilization. Scholars have criticized the Great Books approach for lacking adequate analysis. According to the presupposition of this criticism the classics cannot be seen as speaking to the present reader without an understanding of their historical context.

In the historical-critical method the category of "myth" suffers from this lack of seriousness. Scholars protest that for them "myth" does not mean an untrue story. It may mean that for the vast majority of English-speaking people. For scholars, however, it means simply a narrative generated by the inner experience of a people or a community and told to inculcate a truth, often religious. Thus we can talk about the myth of the Resurrection, the myth of the Incarnation, the myth of the Second Coming, etc.

Such a use of the word "myth" in biblical interpretation raises the difficulty of playfulness. To speak of the "myth of the Resurrection" effectively brackets the question of the reality or truth of the Resurrection. It is neither affirmed nor denied. It is only analyzed as to its meaning. As simply having a particular meaning, it makes no claim on my existence. It summons me to no response, positive or negative. I am asked to look at the steps of a story, not at the impact of the story in my life. It does not require a "yes" or "no" on my part.

The fundamentalist attains seriousness in a very direct way. He simply accepts the massive presupposition that the Bible is written according to the literary forms guiding a modern writer. He thus views the biblical texts as directly addressing the modern reader. As a result fundamentalism allows the reader to participate directly in the subject matter of Scripture.

The second aspect of interpretation deals with the question of coherence. *Historical* criticism has long insisted on the particularity of biblical texts. We must understand a writer only in the light of what he says, not in the light of what another author's statements are. To the careful reader the New Testament consists of clearly diverse teachings. This diversity arises from diverse authors and diverse readers. In the historical critic's eyes biblical texts are occasional writings, writings geared for very particular historical situations. As Leander Keck states, we find in Paul "timely words to concrete situations," not "timeless truths and principles."

The issue of particularity even affects writings produced by the same writer. J. Christiaan Beker refuses to find in Paul any dominant symbol, concept, or essence that would constitute Pauline theology. The "coherent" element in Paul, according to Beker, lies only in an apocalyptic framework within which Paul might say one thing to the Galatians and its opposite to the Romans. Here we see the particularity of Pauline writings not only vis-a-vis other New Testament authors but also within the Pauline corpus isolates one letter from another. Now the idea of reading Scripture conjures up the fish in the bowl trying to listen to a whole aquarium of fish in separate bowls and trying to draw some sense of it all.

Again the fundamentalist attains coherence in a very direct way. He views Scripture as the Word of God. As the revelation of the one God Scripture must all work together. The Bible as a whole must make sense. As the revelation of the one God diverse texts of Scripture can be used to interpret each other. Thus if in the Lord's eyes "a thousand years are like yesterday" (Psalm 90:9), then the seven days of Genesis 1 can be understood as seven thousand years. In the fundamentalist's hands the Bible becomes a treasure of lucid delight, not the tangle of murky contingencies it seems to be in the hands of the historical critic.

Traditional Solutions

Certain forms of traditional Catholicism have attempted to achieve seriousness and coherence by a two-tier approach to theology. Biblical scholars may be allowed to "do their thing." Serious theology, however, is recognized at the level of dogmatics. On this level theology can cohere into a great system and summon a person to a decision about his life. Concerned about the truth of the matter, theology is placed in a separate category in which an institutional authority carefully monitors the results.

The difficulty with this approach lies in the separation of the two moments of theology. Rarely does the dogmatic moment grow organically from the biblical. Magisterial authority becomes the critical element in deciding how a biblical text will or will not summon a believer to a decision. Upon hearing a new biblical interpretation, a Catholic will frequently ask, "But what does the Church teach about this?" In effect an institutional "pre-text" becomes a reference point for determining the serious and coherent teaching of Scripture.

On the other hand, certain forms of traditional Protestantism attempt to seek this biblical truth with its seriousness and coherence by reliance on inner illumination. The inner experience of the heart as the place where the Spirit guides the soul into the truth of Scripture becomes the reference point by which seriousness and coherency arise.

Compared to this inner illumination, all religious language becomes suspect. The mystery of God is placed in such a dialectic with the human intellect that human language, including biblical statements, appears either as childish babblings before awesome incomprehensibility or feeble expressions of religious experience.

When the heart is separated from the head, however, religion becomes radically private. As I listen to another's religious words, I am never sure they express the same inner experience those words evoke in my life. Since my inner experience is the criterion for understanding the truth of my relationship with God, the words of another person cannot really summon me to reform this relationship. In effect a psychological "pre-text" becomes the reference point for determining the truth of Scripture as well as all other religious language.

The Challenge

The attractiveness of fundamentalism in biblical research lies in the way it appears to avoid these "pre-texts" and at the same time affirm its intention to recognize the truth of the Bible in all its seriousness and coherency. By so doing, fundamentalism challenges the historical critic to find the truth value of Scripture as more than its historical meaning.

Most people I know are intensely interested in "the way things really are." A father wants to know if a child is really his child. People want to know if angels, devils, heaven, and hell really exist. Luke portrays Peter liberated from prison as making the distinction between thinking "he was seeing a vision" and "now I am sure" (Acts 12:9-11). This sensitivity lurks behind every concern of illusion or error. I suspect that it is part of the universal human condition.

Lisa Dolittle in *My Fair Lady* protests to her would-be suitor, "Don't talk of love . . . show me." Her protest insists that the truth of the matter lies beyond "the word-event." The power of the truth does not lie in a speaker's or writer's mind or utterance. It lies in the reality that governs the speaker or writer. Fables and myths can be powerful stories but only when they express a dimension of our lives or some other reality. That dimension of life or reality may not be expressable in any other way.

This is not to say that all truthful words are directly informational. In biblical language especially, statements may often lack an exact correspondence in detail to some reality. But words are truthful because they refer to what is other than themselves. Even the four-letter expletive packs its punch because of its intensely concentrated reference to the speaker's state of mind.

Biblical fundamentalism is guided, as James Barr points out, by an intense "didactic emphasis." It looks upon biblical texts as containing teaching or as being teaching. The issue of propositional truth in matters of religion is particularly thorny. Religion deals with realities that necessarily exceed the truth of any human proposition. Decadent scholasticism forgot this and worked out its theological systems by playing with propositions and drawing conclusions from definitions. Reform began when theologians became willing to criticize propositions and definitions against the mystery of religious phenomena.

A blanket refusal of the propositional or didactic in Scripture, however, is a refusal to share biblical truth in a self-conscious, reflective, and therefore critical manner. Experiences are significant or meaningless, but until I make a judgment I am not in contact with reality. Until I express that judgment in a proposition, I cannot share it with others.

Although often aware of the inadequacy of propositions ("I don't know how to say this"), most people I know evidence the importance of statements or propositions. The romanticists I know, furthermore, go out of their way to teach in a multitude of propositions why they hold their position. With this didactic emphasis and zeal to communicate "what the Bible teaches," fundamentalism therefore has a great appeal.

An Alternative: The Rehabilitation of Abstraction

For those who are attracted by the search for serious and coherent religious truth in scriptural texts and unsatisfied with the "pre-texts" described above, what are the alternatives to fundamentalism? In what way can the coherent and universal be found in the particular, the serious in the playful?

If there is to be some discovery of the coherent in the particular, it will have to be by way of abstraction, not the massive abstraction of the fundamentalist drawing a teaching away from all the circumstances in which it was first uttered but a delicate abstraction from circumstances, an abstraction by way of completion.

In the most particular utterances there exists a surplus of meaning beyond the particular historical reason or context of the utterance. The clearest example is that of a presidential address before some particular group. The President of the United States might be speaking to the United Auto Workers, but his words are followed with keen interest around the world for the declarations of public policy they may contain. Far more exists in the address than what the President wishes to say to the labor union.

This example is perhaps of limited value because of the peculiar literary form of a presidential address and the complexity of determining the real audience. But if it were not for the excess of meaning in the subject of the particular proposition, the proposition would say nothing.

Likewise, the christological hymn in Philippians 2:5-11 has a very particular use and meaning in Paul's letter to the Philippians. It functions as a motivator to Christian humility: "Let this mind be in you as was in Christ Jesus" (2:5). But it could not function in this way except by its excess of meaning. It is this excess meaning that can be abstracted as a coherent and serious proposition about Christ.

What any author writes about in a particular historical context is best understood in terms of the situation and questions in the historical audience. However, the historical author would make no sense to anyone except through the excess, which as abstracted from the historical context speaks to all. Paul writes one thing to the Galatians about the Law. The situation and questions of the Galatian community opens up our understanding to what Paul meant to say. But if Paul's statements could not be true for any community, they are false for Galatia and should be recognized as such.

This is not to say that Paul's statements can be simply lifted from a text and applied to life today. What Paul has to say about women, for instance, cannot be separated from Paul's world and the condition of women in that world. What is involved, rather, is a delicate abstraction from the limits and constraints of the historical context, an abstraction that allows Paul's statements to grow into fuller meaning. Despite appearances and even Paul's intention, the excess of meaning in Paul's statements about women might, when abstracted from the historical constraints, express an obligation of intense mutuality and care.

Scripture, like most documents, is in fact a dialogue. In many ways it follows a question-and-answer logic. The answers are best understood by knowing the question, which is usually thoroughly particular and contingent. However, the answer can respond to other questions in addition to the original. It is not the addressing of a new question to a biblical writer and allowing him to answer only with the words used for the original. Rather, the answer can reply to other questions by its excess of meaning. Isaiah never dreamed of the question, "How can humanity avoid destroying itself by nuclear weapons?" But Isaiah's response about beating "swords into plowshares" contains an excess of meaning beyond the one that applied to the Assyrian threat of his time.

Involved in this biblical-theological abstraction is a type of speculative projection, a belief that there is more to the historically bound utterance, that there is a "divine plan" to which the historical bonds belong. As a text is examined along with other texts, a type of abstraction by completion generates a "theme" that "fills in" the speculative projection and eventually includes the original author, the original readers, and the present reader.

This whole process could be called "benevolent interpretation." It involves the "benevolent" presupposition that a larger picture or valid theme does in fact exist beyond the text at hand and the text has a positive relationship to that larger picture. This interpretation follows a critical analysis of the text, but it must skip over the criticism in the expectation of finding truth.

At this point, however, we see the principle difficulty of this method of interpretation. What guarantees the positive relationship of the text to the larger theme? The text might be an expression of error and incapable of expansion in the direction of truth. In the process of "filling in," how does the interpreter know he has moved in the direction of the excess of meaning and not simply read into the texts from an extrinsic pre-text? The further work of the interpreter will verify this probe or projection by either confirming or debunking it.

How do you confirm an interpretation? First of all, the whole process of verification is guided by a deep and personal contemplation of the subject matter. This contemplation presupposes familiarity with the subject matter independent of the text at hand. Eventually, it presupposes contact with the subject matter independent of any text, a contact in contemplative silence.

Second and more specifically, the text must speak to me, and I must be able to relate myself and my life to the text. As an interpreter I begin to overcome the distancing created by objective observation. From being an observer I move to becoming a participant. The verification consists of an experience of oneness between the present reader and the text.

Such a verification seems hopelessly mired in privacy. It operates on the level of inner experience. Hence the third point: To the degree I can communicate that inner experience to others, to the degree I can join others in this view of the subject matter, I rise above subjectivism. I know when I have communicated. But again the experience of successful communication to others remains an inner experience. At the basis of it all is a confidence in the basic experience. This is the fundamental presupposition of serious and coherent biblical interpretation.

Conclusion

I wish only to sketch this method as an alternative to fundamentalism, yet one that takes seriously fundamentalism's fascinating appeal. I have given no "how to's." In fact, I doubt that I have described anything really novel. I would expect most scholarly Christian readers to find here a somewhat abstract reflection of what they are already doing, though they may entertain some doubts about the legitimacy of the process. What I hope to establish is the serious and scientifically honest possibility of biblical theology, the recognition that through this method of interpretation Scripture remains the Word of God. God is revealed in the particular choices of Israel and Jesus.

3
FUNDAMENTALISM'S THEOLOGICAL
CHALLENGE TO THE CHURCHES

Edgar A. Towne

Fundamentalism poses a theological challenge to the churches in the United States because it is an interpretation of Christian faith that appeals to many Christians as well as many others. It has the power to reshape lives. A function of churches is to change persons and societies. In both its liberal and conservative sectors the broad evangelical heritage in the United States has insisted on this from the age of the Puritans through the revivals to the social gospel. No liberal Christian, for example, could consistently disagree with the statement Jerry Falwell unwittingly made to *Penthouse:*

> If I can create a moral climate and consciousness in our state,
> if we can provide such a moral conscience that it is easier for
> politicians to do right than to do wrong, which is not the case
> today, then we have made our contribution.

This statement represents an authentic impulse derived from Christian faith.

Fundamentalism is a theological interpretation of Christian faith whose mainspring conviction is that the Bible is without error in everything that it asserts. Of course, many evangelical Christians share this conviction, but we will focus upon those Christians who desire to be called "fundamentalists" and wear that name proudly. Fundamentalists have also been identified by the intensity with which they hold their convictions. In the American context where religious and moral convictions tend to be privatized and relativized, fundamentalists are often considered fanatics. In this chapter "fundamentalism" is not employed pejoratively but historically to designate a theological interpretation of Christian faith emergent in the Anglo-American sphere during the past century. It is assumed here that religious and moral convictions, if they really are convictions, quite naturally are intensely believed and formative of a person's character and behavior.

Consider the controversial character of the Moral Majority. The public policies of the Moral Majority have received criticism of two major kinds. First, from liberal Christians and from conservative Christians, some of whom are fundamentalists, has come disagreement about the kinds of policies that can be inferred from Christian faith. Many conservatives and fundamentalists do not participate in the Moral Majority because they do not concur in its policies or do not believe that Christian churches should be so explicitly related to politics.

A second major kind of criticism derives from those who appeal not to religious beliefs but to constitutional guarantees of freedom of speech and expression, the separation of church and state, and the resolution of conflict by an orderly democratic process.

Undoubtedly, it is the political influence of the Moral Majority that has drawn the attention of liberal Christians to fundamentalism. To recognize that fundamentalist theology is the motivating power of the political program of the Moral Majority is to testify to the integral relationship among religious convictions, character, and public policy. Falwell never loses sight of the fact that fundamentalist convictions energize his program. These convictions are just under the surface of his public pronouncements, which are stated so as to evoke these convictions. Too often, however, liberal Christians have lost sight of the convictional power of the authentically evangelical beliefs they share with other Christians. They have framed their appeals in terms of rational, constitutional, prudential, or utilitarian arguments. The result is that, though Christian liberals are no less convicted than conservatives, their public face tends to suggest that their own beliefs are relativized or privatized so far as their advocacy in the public sphere is concerned. This has contributed to the belief among fundamentalists that liberals have no faith at all.

Comprehension of the theological interpretation at issue in fundamentalism is important to the nation because differences in belief among conservative, liberal, and fundamentalist Christians inevitably influence their public conduct, thereby influencing the rest of the United States. On a purely demographic basis—apart from astuteness and success in political strategy and tactics—which religions are most popular will be of considerable consequence to the nation's politics. Prevailing beliefs in the churches will also influence the nation's ethos, its characteristic moral tone. This will be true whether the influence is through so-called "private" expression or through the churches as churches. The only alternative is to advocate no influence of religious belief at all in the nation's political life, a patent impossibility barring systematic suppression of religious expression or the disappearance of religious belief altogether in our society. All persons act on their beliefs and convictions, religious or otherwise. So unless great injustice is done to religious persons, it is a "civic virtue" to understand the beliefs prevalent in the churches.

In light of these issues fundamentalism presents a challenging opportunity to the churches to rethink their theology of mission and the style of their public presence. Similarly, the religious right presents a challenging opportunity to both the nation and the churches to develop a philosophy and theology of politics in the context of constitutional democracy and the so-called "wall of separation" between church and state.

The authority of an inerrant Bible tends to displace Jesus as head of the church. This displacement becomes a problematic as it becomes translated into public policies that could influence all of the United States. There is a tendency to describe the authority of the Bible as an inerrant book in a way that eclipses the living divine self-revelation that is claimed as the basis of the Bible itself, the inspiration of its authors by the Holy Spirit (2 Timothy 3:16-17). There is an obvious tension here between an experienced event of revelation and the written expression derivative from that event. To speak of a "tension" need not mean that what is written is false to the event. It does mean that the event cannot be reduced to the written words that witness to it. The event is "concrete" because it is an experienced encounter with God. The biblical witness is "abstract" because it is a type of linguistic expression. The difference between experience and text means that all of the former cannot be conveyed by the latter.

Fundamentalist theology tends to insist on the denial of this difference. When it does so, it tends to think of Christianity as a "doctrine" and not a "life." Instead of saying, for example, that Christianity is a faith life with a doctrine, one says that it must be one or the other. This seems to be happening when J. I. Packer says that "the confession of inerrancy . . . does make a full and faithful articulation of biblical Christianity possible in principle, whereas apart from this confession it is not possible even in principle." The thrust of this statement is that in fact everything that Christianity is is articulated in the Bible and that apart from a belief in its inerrancy it is not possible to know what Christianity is. Once this tendency is realized, it is easy to speak of the *sole* authority of the Bible. The eclipse of the living witness of the Holy Spirit has begun.

Being the sole authority, the Bible must bear a great burden. Its authority must be none other than that of God. The logic of this is displayed in the definition of "inspiration" as plenary and verbal. So it is with "inerrancy," which is claimed not only with respect to salvific knowledge of God true to the essence of Christian faith, but also in respect of everything the Bible asserts. Jerry Falwell's protégés write that fundamentalists "view the Bible as being God-breathed and possessing the quality of being free from error in all its statements and affirmations." They then quote Robert Lightner with approval: "In a book which claims God as its author, inspiration must extend to all its parts." The comprehensive nature of this claim for the Bible is an understandable correlate of the belief that *all* of our knowledge of God derives from the Bible. Yet the claim that the Bible is inerrant in everything it asserts would not seem to be entailed by belief that the Bible is our only source of knowledge of God and salvation. It might be inerrant (or infallible) in these respects but in error in regard to other matters.

Obviously, many Christians are able to live without affirming the Bible's inerrancy in all that it asserts. Fundamentalists, however, are Christians who seem unable to identify themselves as such without belief in an inerrant Bible. These facts suggest that many nonrational, nontheological factors enter into believing. That is certainly to be expected, considering our assumption of the intimate relationship between belief, experience, character, and conduct. Belief in an inerrant Bible is a conviction integral to the identity of fundamentalists without which they would be significantly different people.

Such a claim means at least two things. First, it means that the claim is empirical. The Bible we have in our hands is actually without error. Such a claim is in principle verifiable or falsifiable by some experiential means. Considering the comprehensiveness of the claim, one instance of error suffices to disprove it. To concede just one error is to free oneself from the effort to avoid the "death of a thousand qualifications" (Gilbert Ryle) required to protect the claim from falsification.

Nevertheless, fundamentalists like Paul D. Feinberg take up the effort. He writes, "Although it is indeed a large and heavy burden to have to defend the Bible on all points, it is nevertheless necessary!" The very zeal expended in this effort suggests that there is more to the claim than its empirical dimension. The inerrancy of the Bible is a faith conviction of such persistence that to doubt it is to undermine one's Christian way of being in the world.

However, to defend the claim that the Bible is the sole and inerrant source of our knowledge of God either involves a begging of the question or a basis in knowledge of God now derivative from a source other than the Bible. If the Bible claims inerrancy for itself, as fundamentalist exegesis claims, this is certainly consistent with the claim that it is in all respects so. There is no inner contradiction as in the "liar's paradox."

But to support the claim by adducing a statement from the Bible on the basis of *its* inerrancy because it is part of the Bible is to beg the question. For this appeal not to commit the fallacy, an inference from a knowledge of God's reliability is required. Fundamentalists in fact appeal to this inference, and the tenacity of their conviction suggests that their confidence may ultimately be in God rather than in the book. This is, I think, the basis of any rational and religious plausibility there may be in fundamentalism. For this argument to work both logically and spiritually the inference to the veracity of the biblical text must rest on an immediate knowledge of God as trustworthy not only "back then" when the inspired authors wrote but also now when the claim is made. This is an immediate knowledge of God insofar as it is knowledge of *God.* The intentionality of faith is focused on God and not on the mediation of an inerrant Bible. So far as this is the case in any knowledge of God, it means the Bible is not the sole source of our knowledge of God.

But to the degree that faith's intentionality excludes God in Christ through the Spirit in its knowing, then bibliolatry is embraced.

Of course, fundamentalists would say God is the source of our knowledge of God. The issue, however, is whether it is always a mediated knowledge. Considering their profession of the orthodox doctrine of the perfect humanity and divinity of Jesus as the incarnate Word of God, their appeal to Jesus' view of Scripture is a way of claiming not only that the Bible is inerrant but also that a reliable God endorses it. The way Jesus is appealed to, however, tends to displace the focus of faith from God to the book. So J. I. Packer can write as follows:

> We shall maintain that Jesus Christ constituted Christianity a religion of biblical authority. He is the Church's Lord and Teacher; and he teaches his people by his Spirit through his written Word . . . We shall argue that subjection to the authority of Christ involves subjection to the authority of Scripture. Anything short of unconditional submission to Scripture, therefore, is a kind of impenitence . . . .

We are observing how, as the fundamentalist apologetic proceeds, it builds such a momentum that it holds that since God has actually disclosed himself in part by means of a book that is inerrant, it is *only* by such a book that God is known at all. This is the real fallacy, the *non sequitur*. If, for example, John Calvin committed this fallacy, he would have to be faulted for it, not cited as an authority for it. There is a knowledge of God not mediated by the Bible that is required by the claims made for it, and this creates the theological stresses in fundamentalism.

Having observed in the first stage of our argument a tendency in fundamentalism to regard the Bible as the only source of the knowledge of God, we now turn to the second stage. What occurs in the intentionality of faith when the Bible is used and advocated as the only source of our knowlege of God? Fundamentalist use of the Bible, by which I mean the manner of their appeal ("The Bible says . . . "), tends to inculcate in persons the belief that their knowledge of God is and must be a mediated one. An inerrant Bible is interposed between persons and God much as the church's magisterium was in the Middle Ages. It is a significant difference whether one focuses on God or an inerrant book. Clearly the former is authentic faith and the latter is idolatry. No fundamentalist would countenance idolatry in the form of bibliolatry, and I do not intend to suggest that any fundamentalists do. However, it is a significant difference whether persons understand their knowledge of God to be an immediate one (an "inner light"), a mediated one (through an inerrant Bible alone), or some union of both (the inward testimony of the Holy Spirit). The "inner light" here designates an immediate divine self-communication of the type required by inspiration. The knowledge of God mediated by an inerrant Bible may, of course, include also the influence of persuasive exegesis, reasoning, and preaching. The combination of both is the commonly-acknowledged view of the Protestant Reformers. The knowledge of God intended by the believer as based on the sole authority of the Bible in virtue of its inerrancy is a knowledge the immediate *assurance* of which is the Bible and not God. This is not to be accounted idolatry, but it jeopardizes faith. The stories about the shattered persons whose trust in the Bible has been shaken by their introduction to evolution and biblical criticism are testimony to this empirical jeopardy and its existential significance. This is why fundamentalism in the churches often poses a pastoral challenge.

Third, the tendency in fundamentalism is toward a type of idolatry that involves the displacement of Christ by the Bible as the head of the church. In this regard fundamentalism's challenge to the churches is theological and spiritual. This tendency is observed in a number of doctrinal proposals in favor of inerrancy that depend upon some sort of comparison with Christ. Usually evangelicals have been very careful in their use of these comparisons. They have not always agreed upon their cogency, and I allude to them here only to expose the dynamics of the tendency that culminates in the fundamentalist practice.

An analogy is often advanced that appeals to the doctrinal consensus of the church, that though fully human Jesus was sinless, and to the dogmatic consensus of the perfect union of divine and human natures in the Person of Christ. So Gordon R. Lewis says, "The adaptation of Christ to a human body did not involve sin, and the adaptation of Christ's teachings to human concepts did not involve error." Combined with the analogy to the Person of Christ, an appeal is made to the accommodation in the Incarnation as a necessary condition for the effectiveness of the divine salvific action. J. I. Packer says,

> "God's condescension . . . is one aspect of his saving grace, whereby both in the Son's incarnation and in the Bible's inspiration he brought about a full union and identity of the divine with human, our salvation being his goal."

Packer adds that the unity of divine and human in Scripture must be complete, as it is in Christ. Packer rejects a "kenosis" type of interpretation of the human (accommodated) character of Scripture and of Incarnation because his appeal is to the divine authority of Jesus' own attitude to Scripture in behalf of the complete inerrancy of Scripture.

With respect to this kind of argument B. B. Warfield observed that the analogy of the Person of Christ can be pressed beyond reason. Warfield observed the analogical nature of the comparison of Scripture with Christ and granted a limited value to it.

> There is no hypostatic union between the divine and the human in Scripture; we cannot parallel the "inscripturation" of the Holy Spirit and the incarnation of the Son of God. The Scriptures are merely the product of divine and human forces working together to produce a product in the production of which the human forces work under the initiation and prevalent direction of the divine: the person of our Lord unites in itself divine and human natures, each of which retains its distinctiveness while operating only in relation to the other. Between such diverse things there can exist only a remote analogy; and, in point of fact, the analogy in the present instance amounts to no more than that in both cases divine and human factors are involved, though very differently. In the one they united to constitute a divine-human person, in the other they cooperate to perform a divine-human work.

In the Incarnation the two natures "united." In inspiration they "cooperate." This difference is crucial. Warfield's point is substantially that made earlier, that personhood and language

are not commensurate realities. Warfield nevertheless conclud-
ed that the Scripture is without error. However, without a
hypostatic union of divine and human factors in the Bible inerrancy does not follow from the resulting limited analogy. In his
own way Dewey Beegle has advanced a similar argument. He
attempts to show that God still works through the Holy Spirit
to convict and assure us of the truth of the written Word of
God.

There is a tension in Warfield's own view. The Word of
God written cannot be identical with the living Word of God
encountered in the incarnate Christ or in the Scripture under
the impact of the Holy Spirit. God does not persuade us that
what is not true (a biblical error) is true under the impact of a
belief in the divinity of the Bible. The doctrine of the plenary,
verbal inerrancy of the Bible is not a revealed truth. It is a
theological interpretation. Karl Barth's position that the Bible
uninterpreted is the Word of God respects the dialectic of the
divine and human elements better than that of those who insist
on their interpretation. He argues for "the Bible not yet interpreted, the free Bible which remains free in the face of all interpretation." Unless this dialectic is respected, the application of
the two-natures language of the christological dogma to the
Bible tends to assimilate Christ to the Bible.

In fact, for some fundamentalists Christ is assimilated to
the Bible in such a way that it tends to assume in the believer's
life an authority equal to Christ. The risk is evident in the fact
that inerrantists recognize it. R. C. Sproul writes, "To subordinate the importance of the gospel itself to the importance
of our historical source book of it would be to obscure the cen-
trality of Christ." Nevertheless, some fundamentalists assimilate
Christ to the Bible in such a way that they are all but identified
and the divine Spirit is confined to speaking only through Scripture. This position was encountered by the author when he participated in nineteen one-hour "conversations in contrasting
faith" recorded and broadcast over radio station WNTS in
Indianapolis during 1980 and 1981. Sponsored by the Church
Federation of Greater Indianapolis, the program brought two
mainline pastors and two fundamentalist pastors who were
separatist Baptists together with a moderator.

Both fundamentalist pastors stressed the inerrancy of the

Bible in every area and the intensity of their conviction. In John Hosler's words, "A breakdown in one of these areas would directly affect the plan of salvation in some ways." Greg Dixon said, "Historically a fundamentalist is one who believes the Bible is the Word of God without error, God has the original autographs, he has preserved his Word, and he said what he means and means what he says." Both pastors regarded the inerrancy of the Bible as the basis of their trust in the plan of salvation. When at one point I questioned the claim that Moses was the author of the Pentateuch, Dixon said, "I question whether it is even possible for a man to go to heaven who does not believe that the first five books of the Bible are the words of Moses."

As the conversation developed in one of the two programs devoted to the Bible, the issue I have stressed in this essay emerged, that of the relation of the living Word to the written Word. John Hosler strongly denied that

> there will ever be any variations that we will ever comprehend between the content of the living Word and the content of the written Word. In other words, I don't believe that God's living Word would ever reveal anything to me that I could not through structured analysis demonstrate from the written Word.

The problematic matter here is not that of accurate determination of what the biblical text says. This is the primary task of exegesis. On another program, both men affirmed the principle that the Bible interprets itself and that the meaning of the Bible, in Hosler's words, must "for certain be ascertained." The problematic matter pertains to whether interpretation can be in any sense free from the biblical text as verbally and plenarily inerrant.

In this conversation the issue became explicitly connected to the living Word understood to be the incarnate Christ and his living reality now in the Spirit. It became not a matter of semantic comparisons of meanings and language, but of the difference between the incarnate person of Jesus, the Son of God, and the language bearing witness to him. John Hosler insisted that interpretation could never be an "additional revelation to the Bible," but must be "a direct objective literal understanding of what the Bible is actually saying."

A difference of interpretive principles emerged among us. Dixon and Hosler, as noted above, felt the entire biblical text was the guiding principle of interpretation, I offered our knowledge of God in the incarnate and risen Christ as the guiding principle. To this John Hosler responded significantly:

> The Bible's interpreting of itself is the incarnate Christ. The Bible in its entirety is the product of the incarnate Christ. The incarnate Christ has not chosen to deliver us two Bibles. There's not one Bible in the heart and one Bible on paper. They're both the same Bible. And legitimately I don't believe anybody's heart can produce truth that is not contained in the Bible and call that truth inerrant from God.

Here is the assimilation of Christ to the Bible. While no one should want to claim inerrancy for his or her interpretation, there must be a way in the church for the living Word to challenge all interpretation that appeals to the Bible. This must happen through the "mind of Christ" (Philippians 2:5-8) living by the Spirit in the church. This is not identically the same reality of the incarnate Christ "in the days of his flesh." It is the reality of Christ living in us by the Spirit.

But this also is a different reality from the written words of the Bible. It is this difference that distinguishes the "letter" from the "spirit." It is this difference, when it is respected, that honors the risen Jesus and preserves Christ's headship over the church.

My response to the statement of John Hosler quoted above on the program was as follows:

> Well, I think there's a point up to which I want to agree with John . . . The Bible is an authoritative and reliable witness to who God is. But I would want to say more strongly than John is saying that ultimately the church and every Christian and Christians together must permit God himself to be his own interpreter through the Spirit. It is through the impact of the Holy Spirit when the church's mission is submissive to the Holy Spirit that God will interpret the Scriptures. But the Scriptures present Christ to us, and I believe that revelation is final in the sense that God will not reveal himself to be different from the way he is re-

vealed in Jesus. I think our difference is over how free the Spirit is to speak in words that might not be biblical words.

As I have said, I now think the matter is more than semantic. Fundamentalism displays a tendency not to respect the difference between the written words of the Bible and the inward testimony of the Holy Spirit by which Christ is Lord and head of the church. It is this tendency when actualized that mutes the Christ-informed conscience and subordinates its voice in the church to biblical interpretation.

The fundamentalist use of the Bible tends to make its authority in the life of the believer superior to the internal testimony of the Holy Spirit. This occurs through the altered focus of faith mentioned above, in which trust is transferred from God to the Bible. This inner witness is the convicting witness. When Christ is made subordinate or equal to a Bible, then Christ cannot function as the image and living Word that is transformative in the Christian life (2 Corinthians 3:17-18). In its place is interpretation. It is only by means of this exegesis and interpretation of the *entire* Bible that the mind of Christ and the will of God is known.

An understanding of the plan of salvation that is morally repugnant to a person who believes his or her mind is informed by the mind of Christ is presented by making it *wholly* conditional upon confession of faith in the name of Jesus. Despite the fact that atonement has been made for the sins of the whole world and God's intention is that all may be saved, salvation must await the prayer of repentance in the name of Jesus, for God does not hear and so does not respond to any other prayers. In such a way a fundamentalist interpretation presses the divine compassion and intention into the confines of a "plan."

The point here is twofold. Not only is Christian moral and spiritual criticism of this interpretation cut off. God is also represented as not able to bring the divine salvific intention to fruition in any other way than this because of the conditions God is believed to have bound himself to. This antinomy has been prominent in Christian thought from the beginning.

This theological challenge probes our characters, our attitudes, our actions, and the policies we advocate for public institutions. To grasp this is to see that the fundamentalist challenge to the churches is an intrinsically ethical and moral one. It proposes an interpretation of the gospel and policies derivative from it that are highly problematic spiritually, theologically, and ethically. The problem is that fundamentalist belief and hermeneutic do not permit these issues to be addressed as ethical or as issues of Christian discipleship in which the Spirit might be able to represent the mind of Christ in the dialogue. This may be shown by a brief discussion of fundamentalist views of tensions in the Middle East and the prospect of Armageddon.

It is well known that fundamentalist attitudes toward Israel and tensions in the Middle East are derivative from their interpretation of the Bible. The Bible is understood to predict events that will come to pass in this region preparatory to the return of Christ and the final catastrophe of Armageddon. These events are fixed components of the divine plan. They will come to pass. This is known assuredly on the inerrant authority of the Bible. Were they not to come to pass, the fundamentalist claim would be falsified. The restoration of Israel to its land is an indispensible event in this chain of events. And it *has* come to pass.

Do fundamentalists advocate Israel's right to exist (1) because Israel has a moral or legal right to exist? (2) because God desires its existence? or (3) because the Bible inerrantly requires it as a condition for other events? To the degree that support of Israel is controlled by biblical authority, it is hard to treat this judgment as clearly moral, religious, or legal. The matter is settled entirely by an appeal to the Bible.

In fact, fundamentalist support of Israel becomes so ingenuous that it is highly ambiguous morally and religiously. Jews are part of the divine plan of salvation like the nation Israel. But because they are Jews they, like all other non-Christians, have no part in salvation until they appeal to the name of Jesus and his blood. Fundamentalist theology requires support of Israel's creation by action of the United Nations, which on any other basis fundamentalists would condemn. To the degree that fundamentalists support one policy or another because the Bible says inerrantly that the historical circumstances effected or sustained by that policy will come to pass, the moral and religious quality of that support becomes suspect.

Belief in the sole authority of an inerrant Bible precipitates immense tensions in the Christian's motivation and moral decision making. This can be seen in connection with fundamentalist understandings of the catastrophic events that will accompany the "tribulation" (Mark 13: 3-27) and the battle of Armageddon (Revelation 16: 12-16). What shall be the Christian's attitude toward a war in which human initiatives are required and the divine predestination on the authority of an inerrant Bible guarantees will come to pass? It is hard to see how such a belief permits responsible and rational decision making. On one hand, if you seek to be obedient to the will of God, it is not clear such a war is the will of God. For if the appeal is to the Bible's inerrant prediction of the war, there is only an obedience to the mandate to believe the Bible inerrant. Armageddon may not be the will of God at all. But will Bible-believing Christians not act congruently with their belief in the Bible's inerrancy? That is, will they support whatever policy is consistent with this belief? For the events effected by the policy may be the very events the Bible predicts, thereby verifying the belief.

On the other hand, if you seek to be responsive to your ethical values informed by the mind of Christ (perhaps unawares), you must judge the tribulation and Armageddon evil and protest any policy that will tend to precipitate such events. This requires, of course, a rejection of the fundamentalist interpretive scheme. It is one thing to believe the Bible mandates an apocalyptic catastrophe. It is another thing to claim that the Bible is mandating a catastrophic end because God wills it. The first is a matter of exegesis. The second is a matter of spiritual and ethical commitment. Where is God in this? In the fundamentalist view the Holy Spirit only confirms the truth of the Bible to the heart. The Holy Spirit can hardly speak against the Bible or against exegesis and interpretation. When the Holy Spirit is able in fundamentalism to do so, it is a demonstration of the freedom of the Spirit from the Bible. In these ways the fundamentalist belief in the sole authority of an inerrant Bible subverts a healthy spiritual and moral life grounded in the God of the gospel.

For these reasons it behooves the churches to understand

the dynamic tendencies of fundamentalism to modify the classic theological consensus about the Bible and Christ in a way that is subversive. It behooves all civic-minded persons, especially journalists and politicians, to understand the fundamentalist challenge to the churches and to understand properly the significance of fundamentalism's religious and moral beliefs. To treat them as idiosyncratic or private and to relativize them is to misunderstand the way they function in the fundamentalist's life. Beliefs and convictions are intended in faith to be true. To escape cynicism we require a politics that respects belief and is itself committed. The churches thus render a service not only to God but to the public also.

4
RONALD REAGAN
AND THE EVANGELICALS

Richard V. Pierard

The process of transforming a veteran motion picture star into a President is a remarkable story in recent American political history. Equally interesting is that he is acceptable to conservative Protestants today. At one time virtually all fundamentalists regarded movie attendance as a sin. It was a "worldly" activity in which they simply would not engage. They viewed Hollywood as a moral cesspool, the spiritual fountainhead of evil in America.

This outlook persists in fundamentalist circles even today, although most evangelicals, the moderate wing of conservative Protestantism, no longer consider attendance at the movies to be morally wrong. The fact that Ronald Reagan was a regular fixture on the Hollywood scene for decades should have made him anathema as a presidential candidate in 1980. Yet great numbers of fundamentalists and evangelicals rallied to his support. Many of them believed they were responsible for his victory over President Jimmy Carter. How he wooed and won the evangelicals is the subject of this discussion.

Reagan Becomes a Man of Faith

Ronald Reagan's religious background is rather vague. His father, Jack Reagan, was an indifferent Roman Catholic. His mother, Nellie, belonged to a Disciples of Christ (Christian) church. Ronald was baptized in this church, attended a college related to it (Eureka College in Eureka, Illinois), and listed himself as a member of that denomination during much of his adult life. There is no indication that he attended services regularly or participated in the life of a congregation. As governor of California he occasionally went to the Bel Air Presbyterian Church but did not formally join it. Though it is generally regarded as a society church, its pastor, Donn Moomaw, was nevertheless a committed evangelical. Later Reagan chose him to deliver the prayer at the inaugural in 1981. He did not pray in public or speak often about his religious beliefs, although as governor he customarily attended prayer breakfasts and gave forth the usual expressions of piety expected of elected officials.

His personal life was not marked by the kind of scandals so often evident among Hollywood figures, but it was one that hardly would have evoked admiration in fundamentalist circles. He was divorced and remarried. He became well known as a ladies' man during his bachelor periods, a light drinker, and a teller of off-color jokes. His second wife, Nancy Davis, was the daughter of a wealthy and conservative surgeon. Neither was she known for her religious faith. The four children of his two marriages are scarcely examples of a model Christian family.

Governor Reagan took a moderate stance on what later would be called "family" issues. In 1967 he fired two staff members who were accused of homosexuality. When the story was leaked to the press, he denied this had been the reason in order to protect them. His decision drew a great deal of criticism. Later in 1978, after he was out of office but was now regarded as presidential timber, Reagan came out against the so-called Briggs initiative that would have barred homosexual teachers from public school classrooms. It was defeated.

In his first term as governor he endorsed the Equal Rights Amendment but later changed his stance when conservative opposition mounted. Still, his daughter Maureen was an ERA activist, and he strongly supported statutory changes to end discrimination against women. In 1967 he signed into law a "therapeutic" abortion bill that his own doctor father-in-law urged him to sign, in spite of the antiabortion lobby's efforts to block it. The measure was sufficiently flexible that doctors in California had performed over 60,000 legal abortions by the time Reagan left office in 1975.

And when he reluctantly made his 1979 federal tax return available, it disclosed that he had donated less than one percent of his adjusted gross income to charitable and religious causes. This was hardly a model of Christian stewardship.

In short, Ronald Reagan did not at first glance seem to be the type of person who would be cast as a "born-again" Christian candidate and would serve as the standardbearer of an evangelical "profamily" crusade in 1980. What did make him attractive to so many evangelicals, however, was the conservatism that marked his political outlook. The close identification of American fundamentalists and evangelicals with conservative political and economic views enabled them to overlook the flaws in his character and embrace him as their own.

Assisting in this process was a systematic effort on the part of evangelical conservatives to portray Reagan as a man of faith. This endeavor began during his governorship. An article by William Rose, religion writer for the *Oakland Tribune*, that appeared in the May 1968 *Christian Life* pointed out that at his inaugural on January 3, 1967, Governor Reagan quoted Benjamin Franklin as saying any man who dared to bring the teachings of Jesus Christ into public office would revolutionize the world. He would "try very hard" to bring the precepts of the Prince of Peace to bear in today's world. At a prayer breakfast later that week Reagan said, "Faith in God is absolutely essential if a person is to do his best. Sometimes we're afraid to let people know that we rely on God. Taking this stand just seems to be a logical and proper way to begin." The writer went on to describe how Reagan's mother's faith had a profound impact on him and reported the governor as saying:

> I have spent more time in prayer these past few months than in any previous period I can recall. The everyday demands of this job could leave me with many doubts and fears if it were not for the wisdom and strength that come from these times of prayer.

The pastor from whom he often sought spiritual guidance, Donn Moomaw, commented to the interviewer, "We've spent many hours together on our knees."

Reagan told Rose that he had committed his life into Christ's hands before the election:

> I've always believed there is a certain divine scheme of things. I'm not quite able to explain how my election happened or why I'm here, apart from believing it is part of God's plan for me. I think it is very plain that we are given a certain control of our destiny because we have a chance

to choose. We are given a set of rules or guidelines in the Bible by which to live, and it is up to us to decide whether we will abide by them or not.

Reagan commented to evangelist Billy Graham that "it fills me with terror" to think that seminaries are turning out clergymen who "are more social worker than minister" and that an "entire denomination" teaches "young people to approach their Bible with their own beliefs as to what they should and should not accept." He went on to say that "Christ in his own words gave us reason to accept literally the miracle of his birth and resurrection." We either believe him or must assume "he was the greatest liar who ever lived." If the latter is so, how could such a charlatan have had the impact on the world that Jesus did? The governor insisted that the church's primary responsibility was for our spiritual welfare:

> Jesus was very explicit, it seems to me, about man finding salvation in his own soul, making the determination that he personally would do good. Somehow, it seems, the church is copping out if it substitutes for conversion the coercion of government and the taxing power to make people do good through government programs, whether or not they have made the decision in their own hearts that they want to do good.

To another constituent he wrote, "I could not bear this job for a day if I did not have an abiding faith in God and if I did not feel I could call upon him for help."

The Selling of Reagan to the Evangelicals

The process of warming up American evangelicals to Reagan's possible presidency began soon after he returned to private life. Conservative Republican Congressman John B. Conlan from Arizona, an articulate evangelical with extensive connections, came together with Campus Crusade for Christ leader Bill Bright and other wealthy and influential evangelicals to implement a campaign to elect conservative Christians to public office in 1976. This involved an interlocking network of efforts that centered around Bright's "Christian Embassy" in

Washington, a revitalized right-wing front organization known as the Christian Freedom Foundation, and Third Century Publishers, a firm that put out books and other materials that expressed an ideologically conservative political and economic philosophy allegedly based on biblical principles.

Charismatic talk show host George Otis of Van Nuys, California, elicited the former governor's views on "spiritual and moral issues" in a lengthy interview on his television program "High Adventure." It received wide publicity in the evangelical press and left the distinct impression that he was an evangelical. To Otis, Reagan repeated some statements that were found in the von Damm campaign tract, but he went much further. He condemned the "wave of humanism or hedonism through our land," declared there was a hunger "for a spiritual revival" and "a return to a belief in moral absolutes," committed himself to the "joint venture" to reclaim the principles in the Judeo-Christian tradition by turning America back to God and reasserting our trust in him for national healing, and denounce taking prayer out of the schools as actually the expulsion of God ("I don't think he ever should have been expelled"). He also spoke out against legalizing marijuana, sodomy, explicit sex education, and abortion. On the matter of spiritual renewal Reagan endorsed the view articulated by Otis and almost all other conservative evangelicals that the passage in 2 Chronicles 7:14 ("If my people, which are called by my name, shall humble themselves, and pray, and seek my face, and turn from their wicked ways; then will I hear from heaven, and will forgive their sin, and will heal their land") is applicable to America:

> When you go out across the country and meet the people, you can't help but pray and remind God of that passage in 2 Chronicles, because the people of this country are not beyond redemption. They are good people and I believe this nation has a destiny as yet unfulfilled.

Asked if he had been "born again," the presidential hopeful replied:

> I can't remember a time in my life when I didn't call upon God and hopefully thank him as often as I called upon him.

And yes, in my own experience there came a time when there developed a new relationship with God, and it grew out of need. So, yes, I have had an experience that could be described as "born-again."

As for the Bible, he agreed that it was of "divine origin" because of the prophecies in the Old Testament that "predicted every single facet" of Christ's life. He mentioned a couple of favorite Bible passages, stated that he prayed and received answers to prayers, promised he would seek God's guidance along with the counsel of people in decision making, and agreed he would continue his practice of making decisions on the basis of "what is *morally* right or wrong, not on what was politically advantageous to anyone."

Reagan's bid for the nomination was turned back at the Replublication convention in August, but his credentials with conservative evangelicals were now established. At the same time contacts were made between them and the secular New Right. A close working relationship came into being as the allegedly born-again Baptist Jimmy Carter failed to measure up to their expectations. Resentments over lifestyle changes and the secularization of American society mounted. After drawing first blood in the 1978 senatorial elections, the religious New Right with encouragement from their secular allies formally organized to turn America back to God. With the creation of the Christian Voice, Moral Majority, and the [Religious] Roundtable in 1979, "born-again" politics was now a reality.

Although some in the secular New Right looked to John Connally of Texas as the conservative candidate who would put American back on the right track, most of those in the Christian New Right were hopeful that the aging Reagan would make a bid for the presidency. John Conlan functioned as the coordinator to rally evangelical support.

Meanwhile, a Reagan interview with the anti-Communist Bible smuggler John Bass in 1979 was printed up in tract form as *Ronald Reagan: A Man of Faith* and disseminated among church people. Conlan personally passed out the leaflet at the National Association of Evangelicals Convention in Los Angeles in March 1980. In it the Republican frontrunner called for spiritual renewal in America, and "as a Christian" he pledged to do his share in this venture. The country, he said, is in need of a renewal "that is based on spiritual reconciliation—first with God, then man with man." He also said his favorite Bible verse, John 3:16, meant to him personally "that having accepted Jesus Christ as my Savior, I have God's promise of eternal life in heaven, as well as the abundant life here on earth that he promised to each of us in John 10:10." He went on to endorse the concept of Christian schools and "voluntary prayer" in the public schools and rejected abortion and homosexuality as an acceptable alternative lifestyle. He affirmed that the Bible was of divine origin and that prayer had a central role in his life. He declared that Christians should be involved in politics as a "part of putting Christian principles into practice."

The new Christian Right organizations quickly lined up behind Reagan, although some would have preferred a deeper level of Christian commitment on his part. Richard Zone of Christian Voice said, "Reagan was not the best Christian who ever walked the face of the earth, but we really didn't have a choice." Gary Jarmin, the organization's legislative director, launched a direct mailing campaign and media blitz to generate support for his candidacy. The letters contained quotes from the Otis interview and touted Reagan as "the alternative for the Christian voter who wants to vote a moral Christian man into the highest office in the land." Moral Majority, Inc., was not quite so explicit, and neither did it endorse Reagan formally. Its sympathies were anything but disguised. Jerry Falwell said Reagan was the one candidate he could "swallow" and "the only thing we're waiting for is in our hearts to believe he's a real leader." But before long he had become an unofficial adviser. His executive director, Robert Billings, was hired by the Reagan forces to serve as a liaison with evangelicals. The Moral Majority in Alaska captured the Republican state convention, thereby insuring that the state's delegates would be pledged to Reagan.

All Out for the Evangelical Vote

The time was now ripe for the forerunner to come out publicly and firmly on the evangelical side. His polltaker, Richard Wirthlin, said in May that Reagan had an edge among Protestants who had made a personal commitment to Christ. He expected to keep Carter from "cornering the market" on "born-again" Protestants, who constituted about a third of the population and were significant not only in the South but also in such swing states as Ohio and Illinois. On May 26 Reagan appeared at the Western Desert Gospel Sing in Victorville, California, where at a press conference he was asked whether he considered himself a born-again Christian. After hesitating for a moment he responded:

> Well, I know what many of those who use that term mean by it. But in my own situation it was not in the religion or the church that I was raised in, the Christian Church. But there you were baptized when you yourself decided that you were, as the Bible says, as the Bible puts it, that that is being born again. Within the context of the Bible, yes, by being baptized.

Although many evangelicals would not regard this as a particularly profound statement of faith, and Reagan frankly told an interviewer who had asked him about his religion that "I wouldn't wear it on my sleeve," it was enough to satisfy his sympathizers. Doug and Bill Wead rushed their *Reagan in Pursuit of the Presidency—1980* into print at the end of June in order to court the vote of charismatics and Pentecostals. Christian TV personality Jim Bakker did friendly interviews of the candidate for his PTL Club and his magazine *Action*. TV Evangelist James Robison came out firmly for Reagan in his publication *Life's Answer*, pointing out that Carter's policies conflicted sharply with biblical morality and that the Republican forerunner was a "genuine born-again Christian."

On June 24 some two hundred Protestant pastors from around the state of Georgia assembled in Atlanta's First Baptist Church. They came to hear New Right leader Paul Weyrich and others assail Jimmy Carter's foreign and domestic policies and accuse him of taking "the humanistic side" of every issue that concerned them. They were shown how to organize themselves and their flocks against Carter and for Reagan, and all were given copies of *Ronald Reagan: A Man of Faith*. The result was the formation of the Georgia Pastors Forum, which would work for Reagan's election.

At the Republican convention in July of 1980 Reagan's

evangelical allies influenced the writing of the platform. It came out against the ERA and abortion and called for the selection of only antiabortionists as federal judges. One G.O.P. delegate called it "an evangelical platform." Jerry Falwell was one of those who were called into the nominee's hotel suite to give advice on the selection of his running mate. He warned against the selection of George Bush. However, Bush did agree to support the platform, and before long he too was portrayed as a good Christian. At the close of the acceptance speech Reagan departed from his advance text to make a religious statement that would clearly please the evangelicals:

> Can we doubt that only a divine Providence placed this land, this island of freedom, here as a refuge for all those people in the world who yearn to breathe free? Jews and Christians enduring persecution behind the Iron Curtain; the boat people of Southeast Asia, Cuba, and of Haiti; the victims of drought and famine in Africa, the freedom fighters in Afghanistan, and our own countrymen held in savage captivity.
>
> I'll confess that I've been a little afraid to suggest what I'm going to suggest. I'm more afraid not to. Can we begin our crusade joined together in a moment of silent prayer? [Pause] God bless America.

Reagan had persuaded the more conservative element in his entourage to go along with Bush because the latter had agreed to support the platform. Although Paul Weyrich in a pique of anger at the choice withdrew his personal support from the ticket, there was no sign that the preachers and parishioners of the New Christian Right were particularly upset. Still, Reagan was sufficiently uneasy about their support that he decided to go against the wishes of his advisers and attend the National Affairs Briefing in Dallas on August 22, a New Christian Right promotion orchestrated by the Roundtable.

The risks were enormous, but he turned it into a success. First, he held a private meeting with more than two hundred business and religious leaders in the ballroom of the Dallas Hyatt Regency that included some of the richest men in Texas, such as Nelson Bunker Hunt, T. Cullen Davis, and Eddie Chiles.

After this he held a brief press conference at which he made a statement about the theory of evolution that the media picked up at once:

> I have a great many questions about it. I think that recent discoveries have pointed up great flaws . . . It is a theory, it is a scientific theory only, and it has in recent years been challenged in the world of science, and it is not yet believed in the scientific community to be infallible as it once was believed.

This may have sounded ludicrous but, as Evans and Novak rightly pointed out, it had irrevocably secured the Moral Majority types for the balance of the campaign. He had made the fundamentalists believe that he was one of them in a way that nothing else could have. Since the evolutionists were hardly a viable lobby, it was a political master stroke that cost him virtually nothing.

Reagan repeated nearly all of what he had been saying at an appearance at Coral Ridge Presbyterian Church in Fort Lauderdale, Florida, an evangelical "superchurch." Pastor D. James Kennedy introduced the candidate as "a man who understands the signs of the times and our nation's great traditional principles. Our hope is in God and the promises of his Word. Here is a man who believes that Word, who trusts in the living God and his Son Jesus Christ."

At a press conference before the speech Reagan endorsed creationism, criticized state interference with religion, labeled abortion the taking of human life, and declared he was a "born-again Christian" in the sense that he had once submitted to "voluntary baptism." At a private session with about a dozen evangelical leaders Reagan vowed to appoint "godly men" to positions in his administration because he believed "the government ought to reflect the will of God."

After the Victory: The Evangelicals Ignored

The Christian rightist groups at once claimed they were responsible for Reagan's victory on November 6. They expected to be rewarded with appointments and the implementation of their social agenda. But, as the election results were carefully scrutinized in the following days, it soon became clear that the evangelicals had not been decisive. Reagan's win was due to various factors, most notably the economy, the desire for a change, cynicism about politics and government in general, and the widespread perception of Jimmy Carter as an ineffective leader. One could see from remarks made at his first press conference on November 6 as president-elect that he was already preparing to distance himself from the Christian right. He promised nothing to the New Christian Right.

> I have told the people who have supported us in this campaign that I'm going to do as I did when I was governor of California—that I'm going to be open to these people. You want a President of all the people, and I am going to want to seek advice where I think that I can get advice from those who are familiar with a particular problem.

This was clear in his appointments. Only one major New Christian Rightist was given a post, Bob Billings as Assistant Secretary of Education for Nonpublic Schools. He was soon eased out of this job when protests mounted from Catholic educators. Presidential counselor Edwin Meese III came from a family of Missouri Synod Lutheran pastors. He remained an active Lutheran and was regarded by some as "born-again." But he never identified with the Christian Right. Two other evangelicals named to high positions, Dr. C. Everett Koop, Surgeon-General, and James Watt, Secretary of the Interior, were conservatives but neither was associated with the New Right. Reagan's first woman appointee to the Supreme Court, Sandra Day O'Connor, was opposed by the Christian Right because her record on abortion in their judgment was not perfect.

Nellie Gray, one of the leading activists in the prolife movement was outraged because Reagan declined to participate in the March of Life on January 22 (she called this his "first broken promise"). She was not mollified when he invited its leaders into the Oval Office for a brief chat. To be sure, it was the first private meeting of the President with a special interest group, but it was largely a ceremonial and symbolic act.

The real significance was pointed out to journalist Lou Cannon by a White House aide. He warned the writer not to make judgments until he saw what the Administration actually gave the Moral Majority and its allies.

"What do you want to give them?" Cannon asked.

"Symbolism" was the reply.

He then offered an analogy from the film *The Godfather* in which the leader advises, "Hold your friends close, hold your enemies closer." This was the tactic the Administration would follow with its friends on the right. "We want to keep the Moral Majority types so close to us they can't move their arms."

Reagan did send up a prayer amendment and tuition tax credit bill to the Hill and argued for an antiabortion amendment. But the primary emphasis during the Administration's first two years was on economic and defense programs. Pollster Richard Wirthlin told him frankly that matters like abortion, busing, and school prayer were "no-win issues" as far as the Administration and the Republican party were concerned. It was important "in terms of his constituency" for Reagan to reiterate his views on social issues, but actually doing anything about them would not be "helpful to the President." He was very much in favor of school prayer but did not argue its case as strongly as other priority legislation.

Still, Reagan felt a need to keep lines open to the evangelicals, and his liaison with religious groups, Morton Blackwell, admitted that Bill Bright, Jimmy Draper (current Southern Baptist Convention president), Adrian Rogers, Jerry Falwell, and Pat Robertson ("700 Club" host) met frequently with him.

Courting the Evangelicals Again

In September 1982 the President made a dramatic appeal to religious thinking in the Landon Lecture at Kansas State University in Manhattan. Once again he used all the "God words" and phrases that had been so much a part of his earlier expressions of religiosity. He forcefully pleaded for the social agenda of the New Right, renewed military strength to save the world from Communism, and a prayer amendment to put God back in the schools. At the end of January 1983 he gave a tub-thumping speech at the Washington convention of the National Religious Broadcasters where he repeated the Dallas statement. He said the First Amendment was written to protect the people and their laws from government tyranny, not religious values.

He also criticized federal court decisions on prayer. He promised to continue to submit a prayer amendment and advocate tuition tax credits. He would continually lament the suffering endured by unborn, aborted infants.

Then in March the Chief Executive journeyed to Orlando, Florida, to address the National Association of Evangelicals and delivered what journalists quickly labeled the "evil empire speech." He condemned the "totalitarian darkness" of the Soviet Union, called for a rejection of the nuclear freeze proposal, and reaffirmed the package of social issues his audience saw as important. The outrage that swept the media revealed it to be the most noteworthy religious statement he had made to date in his presidency. The NAE's Robert Dugan, however, defended this as the President's expression of "sincere religious beliefs" and said his "seeking to translate his deepest convictions into political positions [is] something we've been trying to get evangelicals to do."

In 1983 Reagan did other things as well that could be interpreted as serving to curry evangelical favor. At the National Prayer Breakfast on February 3 he signed a proclamation officially declaring 1983 "The Year of the Bible" and agreed to serve as Honorary Chairman of the National Committee for this event. The chairman was none other than Campus Crusade's Bill Bright. On February 23 he presented the Presidential Medal of Freedom to Evangelist Billy Graham, the first living Protestant clergyman ever to receive the highest civil award of the American government. (Martin Luther King had been given it posthumously.) He lauded Graham for being "one of the most inspirational spiritual leaders of the twentieth century" and said he "is an American who lives first and always for his fellow citizens. In honoring him, we give thanks for God's great spiritual gifts—faith, hope, and love."

Although it was not so clear in 1981, two years later President Reagan was obviously quite concerned about the social issues that had drawn evangelicals into his circle. In spite of some disgruntlement in the Christian Right camp about Reagan's lackluster performance in achieving its social objectives, one could still expect a strong effort on its part to secure his reelection.

It is no wonder, then, that in early 1984 the movie actor

President from California came out with both guns blazing. On January 13 he issued a proclamation declaring January 22 as "National Sanctity of Human Life Day," and it was widely distributed by antiabortion groups. His State of the Union address on January 25 affirmed the idea of "spiritual revival" and "a crusade for renewal" and insisted the "American dream" was "keeping faith with the mighty spirit of free people under God." He promised to press for tuition tax credits for people who send their children to private schools, endorsed the school prayer concept, condemned child pornography, and reaffirmed his support of efforts "to restore protection of the law to unborn children." Four days later in his formal statement that he would seek reelection, Reagan included the comment, "We have more to do in.... seeing if we can't find room in our schools for God."

The President also appealed directly to evangelicals with stirring speeches before their national meetings. He addressed groups like the National Religious Broadcasters and the National Association of Evangelicals.

To help rally evangelical support for the President's reelection, a quarter of a million copies of a minibook written by Reagan on abortion were distributed. Another several thousand copies of a campaign biography entitled *Reagan Inside Out* by Bob Slosser were peddled throughout the country.

At the Republican convention he highlighted the "religious issue" at a massive prayer breakfast, and it occupied a central place in the ensuing election campaign. Not since 1928 had a presidential candidate placed so much emphasis on religious matters, and it evoked enormous controversy as the campaign wore on, although it was hardly decisive in Reagan's victory.

Conclusion

It is patently obvious that Ronald Reagan has used evangelicals for his own purposes. Perhaps the best description of what has transpired came from the pen of Martin Marty. He called attention to the "pathetic" response of the NRB evangelicals to the President's invective against abortion and plea for school prayer and commented:

The broadcasters evidence nothing, nothing at all, distinctive in their program. They represent a mere fanaticization of the Reagan administration's secular causes. They could not do more than peep about his instituting a Vatican ambassadorship, so flattered were these being-used folks that a President was using them.

Fanaticization? These heirs of biblical prophets of peace want more than bombs, more militancy than even the administration does. They want more intensity against abortion than Reagan puts into action. The Baptists among them, forgetting what their foreparents died for, suddenly want to have the government do for them what theocratic governments used to do for those who squelched their ancestors: establish a form of religion through constitutional amendments promoting "voluntary" school prayer.

Still, President Reagan does have a sincere personal faith, and of course he has the same right as any American to hold and express his beliefs publicly. It would be unfair to see it as mere hypocrisy. Marty's phrase "sincere but inauthentic" is more apropos. In other words, putting the hoopla of his evangelical boosters aside, we may legitimately question his understanding of Christianity. Is it a profound, deep, and meaningful faith, or is it some sort of Eisenhoweresque civil religion?

His courting of the evangelicals indicates that a political dimension to his religious commitment definitely exists. But is that really Christianity in the sense that the church has traditionally regarded it? It appears that the intrinsic difference between the President's faith and that of his evangelical admirers is substantially greater than the latter understand or would care to admit.

He has used them, but is the relationship really a symbiotic one? Will they be able to utilize his help in spreading the gospel message and reestablishing Christian moral values in this secular land? If the divergence between his faith and theirs is really as great as this writer believes it to be, then that is doubtful. What will result is simply a politicized Christianity that deviates widely from the New Testament ideal. Like Esau of old the evangelicals will eventually discover they have sold their spiritual birthright for a bowl of conservative lentil soup.

5
THE ELECTRONIC CHURCH

Angela Ann Zukowski, MHSH

Television has become the principal medium of mass communication and mass information. It has brought about a major revolution in the development of our lifestyle, culture, religious perspectives, and social habits. As is so often the case with revolutionary developments in technology, television originally was regarded as no more than a toy, a minor innovation in the art of popular entertainment, not deserving to be taken seriously. Now television is becoming a ubiquitous, highly influential force in our society. It is not surprising, therefore, to find that "the fundamentalist upheavals that have shaken large parts of the world seem to have found an echo in the rise of the 'electronic church' on American television" (Annenberg and Gallup Research, 1984).

A generalized critique of the electronic church should not be divorced from an assessment of the effect of television on the modern world. Knowledge of the effects of television on our lives lags far behind the current critique. What is critically needed at this time is a discussion of the meaning, place, and future direction of theology, religion, and the church and their relationship to the newer technology.

One of the first media scholars to study the impact of TV on the culture was Marshal McLuhan. His famous slogan was repeated so frequently as to become the hallmark of the TV era: "The medium is the message." Basically, what McLuhan said was that TV had changed the fundamental way in which we perceive reality. We were now able to see and hear what is happening in other parts of the world almost immediately. In the past we were limited to the newsprint media for our information. Now television brought the news into our homes. We live in a new information era in which reasoning is being replaced by an image-oriented type of perception and thinking. This change in the structure of human perception may change the way we look at the world, society, culture, and religion.

Studies have recently been made to determine the impact of television on both the individual and the society. A growing number of organizations such as ACTA (Action for Children's Television) and TAT (Television Awareness Training) have been formed to assess both the content and the format of programs aired on our networks. Books and articles discuss the impact of television on our lives. For example, Robert Alley in *Television: Ethics for Hire* describes television production and its motivation and intentions:

> Television may have many practical uses, but its primary character lies in two areas: as a conveyor of information and as an artistic medium, a maker as well as a reflector of cultures.

Even though programming may attempt to communicate facts, all programming must also reflect the experience and convictions of the communicator. Viewers need to develop skills so they can interact critically with television programming.

Does television reflect or create our culture? Stewart M. Hoover in *The Electronic Giant* states:

> Television as an issue is difficult to grasp because it is both an institution of society and a pervasive experience in which all share. Because it is a pervasive experience, part of television's role is to inform the viewer, part of it is to train the viewer to be informed. Because it is both an institution and an experience, the distinction is made clear between an institution from which certain information comes and an institution that creates a framework for evaluating that information.

Hoover calls television a "dubious authority" that needs to be challenged. The more engaged we become with the television medium in a truly discriminating manner, the more effective we can become in dialoguing with the political, social, and religious world views of the larger community. No matter what we think of television or how the electronic church uses it, current surveys indicate that television does influence the viewer. George Gerbner suggests that a discrepancy exists between how viewers think television affects them and how it does affect them: "What a viewer learns and what a community absorbs over time are far different things." Television is important for what it

> contributes to the meaning of all that is done, a more fundamental and ultimately more decisive process. The consequence of mass communication should be sought in the relationships between mass produced and technologically mediated message systems and the broad, common terms of image cultivation in a culture.

How does television viewing affect us personally and communally? Gerbner believes that it influences us in both ways, depending on how much time we spend in front of the TV set:

> We have found that the amount of exposure to television is an important indicator of the strength of its contribution to the ways of thinking and acting. For heavy viewers, television virtually monopolizes and subsumes other sources of information, ideas and consciousness.

The amount of time people spend watching television is astounding. Over 98 percent of all homes had at least one working television set in 1980, and 49 percent of those homes have at least one color set. Over ten million television sets are sold each year in the United States alone. According to recent figures, the average adult watches two-and-one-half hours per day. Children twelve and under watch slightly more. And the average set is on nearly seven hours a day.

In the future television will play an even more significant role. Cable television with its multichanneled systems, the interactive home television system, the interfacing of technology, television, microcomputers, and digited elements, and satellites to eliminate most distance transmission problems have combined to break down the boundaries between print and the electronic media and between work, education, religion, and leisure activities.

The phenomenal success of the electronic church in recent years is best understood by coming to grips with the reality that evangelical faith has indeed been a persistent and significant component of American culture. For many years liberal Protestant establishments treated evangelical religion as though it were an archaic religious form peculiarly persistent in some regions of the country but not significant in American culture.

George Gallup declared 1976 "the year of the evangelical." What that date really symbolized was the nonevangelicals' discovery that this sector of American society was very large. Perhaps it was also a turning point for evangelicals, who found that their world view was shared by a far larger proportion of American society than they had previously imagined.

Contributing to the success of the electronic church is the national malaise ever since the assassination of John F. Kennedy. We lost our leader. We lost a war that had torn us apart at home. We lost confidence in business and government. A President once admired by millions left office in disgrace. Inflation soars. Energy is scarce. International tensions mount. The fear of a world holocaust is more prevalent than ever before. Many who are in their forties and fifties are witnessing the radical changes in values and lifestyles of their peers and children.

The electronic church united a new counterculture in the United States, one grimly determined to halt the spread of liberal, laissez-faire attitudes and policies in society, culture, and government. The counterculture movement of the 1960s pushed America toward the left, the counter-counterculture of the electronic church is pushing equally hard to the right. The electronic church with its prominent television ministries expresses a fairly stable, coherent, and conservative world view that serves more to rally believers than to recruit or convert others. Its regular viewers tend to be older, more "fundamentalist," and lower in income and education than nonviewers. For them, watching religious television is an expression of belief and an experience that is not inconsistent with, and may even complement, local church attendance (Annenberg and Gallup Research).

The message of the electronic church is comforting to many and challenging to others. There is virtually no home in the United States into which the electronic church cannot send its songs, sermons, and appeals in generous measure. It has brought to millions of Americans a new way of experiencing religion. In fundamental ways the electronic religious experience is affecting the manner in which those same millions view and understand the world in which they live. It offers individuals and families meaning and certainty while other TV programs continue to present more bad news, crime, and dramas that seem to condone lifestyles and language that affront traditional value systems.

The electronic church's success reflects the cultural drift—some would say stampede—toward conservatism. Financially, since there is such a large population of evangelical Christians in our society, even modest contributions from a small proportion of them can sustain fairly extensive broadcasting. Culturally, large segments of our population are ready for change. Conservative political and economic views have much greater credibility than at any time since before the Great Depression. The electronic evangelists offer something that works, something to believe in.

Whatever else one may think of them, the evangelical broadcasters have thrust the church into the electronic age. Their aggressive use of television, communication satellites, computers, and mass marketing practices has implications with which the church is still grappling. The escalation of production and broadcasting costs has forced the electronic church to explore means for generating income. The computer has offered them the ability to target direct mail, poll its constituency, and put out reams of advertising and public relations copy. The electronic church now has the tools to generate both members and dollars. The computer can acquire, sort, store, and retrieve increasing amounts of information about people on mailing lists with accelerating speed and sharply declining unit cost. As the electronic church builds up its data bank, information is gained from the intimate personal problems of those who appeal to it and its counseling services for help. This information in turn becomes a basis for further fundraising. Dangers inhere in this combination of power through money and knowledge.

It would be good to have a little theological breathing space in which to consider some of these implications. The futuristic scenarios in technological communication that once were the stuff of science fiction are rapidly becoming present realities, and evangelical broadcasters are just as quickly adapting them to their purposes. Yet they have not demonstrated a corresponding aptitude for justifying theologically the validity of their enterprise and the compromises that have been made to adapt to the demands of these new technologies. For example, the manner in which the televangelists sell their message conforms to the logic of television, whose stock in trade is an endless stream of easy answers to difficult questions. The most difficult human problems are brought to satisfactory resolution in thirty to sixty minutes. A lot of people believe their favorite televangelists really do answer their mail personally. But for the church as a whole a theological evaluation of the promise and dangers of electronic technology is critical. As human society rapidly becomes an extended electronic network, it is imperative that the church's response be guided by clear theological insights and not mere opportunism.

While it is unlikely that the electronic world will stop while the theologians get on, a valuable historical perspective has recently emerged, one that offers the opportunity to evaluate the effectiveness of current Christian media. Trends in the syndication and audiences of evangelical television programs over the past few years indicate that the much-heralded development of the evangelical use of television has reached its peak. Christian broadcasting as a whole now stands at a crossroads and is poised to move in a new direction.

Audience figures gathered for the past ten years indicate that the combined audience size for all syndicated religious programs reached a growth peak in 1977-78. This pattern is reflected in both Arbitron and Neilsen audience survey figures. Since then the combined audience of these programs has been fluctuating, but it is still below the 1978 level. It appears that religious television shows have reached the point at which they are now largely attracting the segment of the total television population that is going to be attracted by the present format and content. While there has been some movement in the size of audiences for different programs (some have been increasing while others have been decreasing), the total combined audience for all programs reflects the saturation point.

This marketing reality has several implications for religious broadcasting as a whole. It places us in a position from which we can begin to evaluate the effectiveness of the evangelical broadcasting strategy. In the spring of 1984 the results of a research project on religion and television conducted by the Annenberg School of Communications at the University of Pennsylvania and the Gallup organization were released. The project was commissioned by thirty mainline and independent church groups. The purpose of the research was to analyze the content of religious programs on television, and survey viewers of religious and other programs. The research indicated that evangelical broadcasting has become a specialized programming service for a specialized audience. The overwhelming majority of the regular audience of evangelical television programs are people who are already evangelical Christians, further distinguished by other, more specialized, characteristics such as frequent use of Scripture and other devotional materials, regular attendance at midweek as well as Sunday church activities and meetings, and residence in Southern states. The research goes on to state:

> The audience for religious programs on television is not an essentially new, or young, or varied audience. Viewers of religious programs are by and large also the believers, the churchgoers, the contributors . . . . It appears to be an expression, confirmation, and cultivation of a set of religious beliefs and not a substitute for them.

The development of the electronic church, its dominance by evangelicals, and the reasons for its recent phenomenal success are to be seen as part of the electronic communications revolution. Neither the technology nor its application is unique to the electronic church; rather, it is in fairly extensive use in many sectors of our society.

If the danger in the electronic media is the pure consumption of images, then electronic religion can easily become a pushbutton spiritual gratification, mere appearance, and instant release, bypassing a real, personal commitment lived out in everyday life, a physical and social contact with other believers, involvement in a local church community, and outreach to others. If religious groups use the mass media to build barriers to the Christian faith or water down the Christian faith for mass consumption, we must challenge its authenticity.

Avery Dulles has said:

The more I think about the matter, the more convinced I become that communications are a part of what the church is all about. The church exists in order to bring people into communion with God and, thereby, to open them to communication with each other. If communications is seen as the procedure by which communion is achieved and maintained, we may also say that the church *is* communications. It is a vast communications network, designed to bring people out of their isolation and estrangement, and to bring them individually and corporately into communion with God, in Christ.

Yes, the "church is all about communications." It needs to find the most creative means of using the new technologies to assist in bringing people out of their isolation and estrangement. The new procedures and methodologies will not be handed to us. We need to discover and create them. We must design our programming in categories of people to whom the church ministers, not in categories of technology. It is an inversion of thinking to allow the tools and the technology to dictate our priorities.

In the document entitled "Pastoral Instruction on the Means of Social Communication," the bishops of the Catholic Church stated:

Religious programs that utilize all the resources of radio and television enrich people's religious life and create new bonds between the faithful. They help in religious education and in the church's active commitment in the world. They are bonds of union for those who cannot share physically in the life of the church because of their sickness or old age. In addition they create new relationships between the faithful and those people—and today they are legion—who have no affiliation with any church and yet subconsciously seek spiritual nourishment . . . . The church cannot afford to ignore such opportunities. On the contrary, she will make the fullest use of any fresh opportunities that the improvement of those instruments may disclose.

6
STANDING FIRM IN AN EARTHQUAKE: FUNDAMENTALISM, PLURALISM, AND POLITICS

Peggy Ann Leu Shriver

In the course of reading about the religious New Right, I ran across a recent analysis by *New York Times* correspondent Thomas L. Friedman:

> (An) acute sense of national crisis and political drift was compounded by the social dislocations taking place in the nation. Thousands of people moved from the small towns and farms to the cities searching for work opportunities and advancement, but such things were as scarce as a home to live in. . . .
>
> "People were looking for a sense of direction," said (one novelist). "My own son tried everything, Communism, socialism, liberalism. Now he has come back to his own faith. His basic argument was that the country had lost its way because it adopted alien lifestyles and that both the indivdual and the state can only find their real identity through a return to religion. . . . "
>
> While there are no precise figures on how many citizens were caught up in this movement . . . sociologists estimate it to be 20 percent of the people, largely among the cities' middle and lower middle classes.
>
> In the early 1970s this religious orientation began to crystallize into associations grouped around charismatic prayer leaders, or in neighborhoods, small towns, or college campuses. They provided prayer sesssions, publications, and the warmth of a surrogate family . . . .
>
> We are talking here about a very potent political force, (an American University sociologist) acknowledges. It is not threatening the state right now, but it is the most serious of all opposition groups in the country.

I was nodding my head in agreement with this journalist when I was startled to discover that this was not a description of the United States, but a report of the rise of militant Islamic fundamentalism in Egypt. What this suggests to me is that the rapid changes in modern society have provoked some similar responses throughout the world as people try to regain their footing in a time of upheaval. None of us is immune from some sense of vertigo. The response of fundamentalist Christians to these rapid shifts in values has been particularly noticeable and troubling. The aim of this discussion is to attempt to understand this fundamentalist response.

There is a gross presumption on the part of this liberal evangelical in thinking that she can speak about the beliefs and behavior of fundamentalists when there are surely thousands within a few miles of each of us. By practicing empathy, using statistics and studies from the social sciences, and recognizing my own limitations, I will humbly attempt to do it. Indeed, the very effort of trying to put oneself in the position of stating the case for someone else is painfully instructive. As Rapoport in his book *Fights, Games, and Debates* urges, it is important in any argument to be able to state the position of the other side for the benefit of the other side's satisfaction before moving into the next stage of debate.

But there is a more deeply religious reason that Don W. Shriver expressed very forcefully in a speech on pluralism, and I feel constrained to quote it:

> Jesus knew that what mattered—what was unnegotiable about his relation to us—was the relationship itself. To maintain it he prayed forgiveness for whatever in us was willing to destroy it. . . . And we Christians who have less reason to be so sure of our knowledge of the unnegotiably human, who nonetheless do believe in some notions of right without which we might be even less human than we are—what higher obligation can we have than that of not letting our knowledge of good and evil divide us from our brothers and sisters? If the knowledge proves to be defective, as it most probably will, we shall have maintained our relationship to our brother and sister. If it proves to be truly human, we shall have the relationship in which that proof may be enjoyed.

One of the spiritual disciplines of writing *The Bible Vote* has been the attempt to put myself vicariously into the place of the fundamentalists whom we tend to lump into the unfortunate category "Moral Majority." I've studied many of their documents, letters, papers, and television shows and have read background books such as George Marsden's *Fundamentalism and American Culture.* But to avoid academic pretense and to risk some imprecision, let me speak in the first-person composite role of a hypothetical but in many respects very "real" fundamentalist:

I don't know what's come over this country in recent years. I love America and am proud to be an American, and I'm not sorry my grandparents came over here. But we have got to get this country back on track, make it a Christian nation once again, the way our forefathers meant it to be. We used to be a Bible-believing people until the liberals got hold of it and tore it up with all their so-called "higher criticism" that nobody knows what part to believe anymore.

I hold the liberals and secular humanists responsible for a lot that has gone wrong in this country. They won't let our kids read the Bible or pray in school. They teach this "values education" stuff that turns a kid loose to do and think whatever he pleases. All this in the name of religious liberty.

I believe in religious liberty, myself, but that doesn't mean religion should be left out of things. That's not what's intended by "separation of church and state." I've not been much of a person to get involved in politics, but it's time some of us God-fearing folk stood up and put things back to rights.

I look to the Bible for what's right. It's all written there, plain for anyone with common sense to see. God meant everybody to be able to read it and see the truth, with or without much education. He didn't mean only educated people with fancy degrees could be saved, but, praise the Lord, he can use them, too, to witness to the unchanging truth of his Word. That Bible is the source book for our understanding about everything. From it we can use the scientific method of deduction to know whatever we need to know about the world.

Some scientists today ignore the most basic "facts" available—the Bible itself. They think they are really scientists! Especially the evolutionists. I know that people made a fool of us over the Scopes trial back in the twenties, trying to turn us all into backwoods local yokels, but we know better. Now the scientists are beginning to look pretty silly—look what a mess they've gotten us into by not taking the Bible facts as seriously as nature. It's no wonder our kids behave wild. They can't have any self-respect if they're told they are nothing but advanced monkeys! "Treat 'em like animals and they will act like animals," my preacher says.

It used to be that you could count on the public school to teach Christian values but, thanks to the liberals and humanists, you can't anymore. We have to set up our own schools. That costs a pretty penny, but we have to get rid of the teachers and textbooks that are undermining our country's faith and morals. Fortunately, we have some good colleges and lots of Bible colleges we can send our children to, and they can be a part of a Campus Crusade program or Youth for Christ fellowship.

But you can send your children to all the Christian schools you want, and you still have to contend with television. It's time we got rid of the moral pollution on the TV. It has gotten so bad I'll wager even some of the liberals have had a stomach full of those raunchy blue jeans ads! We're doing a boycott on businesses that pay for some of that sex and bad language and even promotion of homosexuality. That isn't a curb on freedom of speech—it is simple marketplace supply and demand. We don't like what they are supplying—and we are cutting off demand. It is a sad day in this country when freedom of speech means freedom to use bad language and tell off-color stories!

I have a great vision for this nation, but I think lots of people have lost it. This country was set up on Christian lines. Democracy is a Christian form of government, giving every person a say. As a Christian nation America can lead the rest of the world into democracy and Christianity. We had the strength and moral courage to do it—or at least we used to—and we can again. God has made us the New Israel, a city set on a hill, a beacon to the world. We have an obligation to all humanity, and the eyes of the world are upon us, so that other nations will become Christian, too.

That means we must be militarily strong. The forces of evil constantly try to pull down God's chosen ones. My preacher says that Russia and Communism are the anti-Christ, that the tribulation is almost upon us, and it probably means a nuclear war. But if we are right with God, we can be raptured to heaven and not endure the Tribulation. Then Jesus will come, and the millennium.

Now I know that not all preachers agree on this. Some are dispensationalists. Some believe in posttribulation instead of pretribulation. Others are millennialists, but they don't seem very sure about the timing.

Some of my millennialist friends don't see any point to taking any political action because things are going to get worse until the Second Coming anyway. But I still have this vision about America. I think we ought to keep trying to strive for the coming of the kingdom and witness to Jesus wherever we can so that when he comes again, we will be ready.

Sometimes places like New York City seem more like Babylon than the new Israel. We've got to witness against sin wherever we find it. My postmillennialist neighbors think God and Satan are struggling all right, and that God is sure to win, but I don't see the golden age they keep talking about. I do rejoice in the Jews' return to Israel, though. That is a sign that Jesus will be coming soon.

You can tell churches that are loose in doctrine by noticing where they stand on moral issues and whether they indulge in worldly behavior. The two go together. The liberals don't have firm beliefs about the Bible, so they don't have witnessing power, and their moral behavior shows they have not been born again. Along with the secular humanists they are stamping on the values of the rest of us. Moral decay is corrupting our country.

Our families are being destroyed. If we don't save the family, which is the cornerstone of American society, the whole country may fall. Just think of what is happening in many American households today. Children talk back to their parents. Sons or daughters run off and live together brazenly. Drugs and alcohol are used so much by the parents that the kids don't need outside teachers. And our own government has legalized many of the things historic Christianity has declared to be immoral and evil so that our children are confused.

One of the worst things that is happening is that girls no longer know what it is to grow up to be women. Now isn't that ridiculous? Of all the things to be confused about, one ought at least to know the God-given place of a woman as a support and helpmate to her husband. This ERA business is the cause of a lot of our family troubles. I can't think of a cleverer way for Satan to infiltrate this country than through the secular humanist's undermining of the family, whether it's supporting ERA or promoting homosexuality, abortion, or pornography.

Frankly, I don't understand the flabby-minded folk who call themselves Christians but who keep thinking that the world is changing, values are changing, and their religious understanding is changing. I think some of them even think God himself is changing!

God's truth is given once-and-for-all through the Bible. Those who see the truth as changing are just trying to take hard truth and make it soft so they don't have to strain to obey it. They are even trying to rewrite the Bible to suit themselves! We need to return to the Bible, to the fundamental facts of Jesus' virgin birth, the substitutionary atonement, Jesus' bodily resurrection, the authenticity of the miracles, and the inerrancy of Scripture. On these five fundamentals I stand, and there is no changing them. It is all common sense, and it is all in the Bible. I pity the people who haven't heard the word of salvation, but I condemn those who have heard and who preach a false doctrine!

From this monologue I hope we have gained an insight into the feelings of fundamentalists. It is a distinct way of viewing the world, a paradigm in conflict with other paradigms. George Marsden in *Fundamentalism and American Culture* asks—but does not answer—a basic question: "Should Christianity and the Bible be viewed through the lens of cultural development, or should culture be viewed through the lens of Scripture?" The fundamentalist will quickly answer that a true Christian views culture through the lens of Scripture.

We have, therefore, a basic conflict that will haunt every effort to understand and communicate with one another. Another way of stating the issue is to ask a pair of questions: Is God's truth solely in Scripture, available to the common sense reader, unchanging in its perceived message? Or does God speak to us in many ways: through Scripture, through the church as the body of Christ wrestling with its understanding and response to God in a particular historical moment, through a use of secular forces such as other nations in the Old Testament, through the voices of the outcast, through other cultures and nature? My choice of this pair of questions is obvious as I ask another question: Do our perceptions of the Bible change as our knowledge of the world and the universe changes and our awareness of the way Scripture was put together and handed on to us? This is not the time nor place, however, to give a full explication of these different ways of hearing God's voice in the world today.

For the fundamentalist I have a further question: If the truth in Scripture is so self-evident to common sense, why have so many people failed to see it? And a question also for liberals: Can truth bring solace, commitment, and security if our understanding is constantly undergoing revision? Beware lest our understanding of God become a substitute for God—so that the limits of human faith foster idolatry. Each of us selects from the Bible passages that have special meaning for us and tends to ignore passages that are disturbing to our conception of God and divine action in the world. This selectivity composes our own private "canon" of Scripture. We in the church need one another to challenge our personal selectivity for its self-serving bias.

Fundamentalists have their private canon, too, while claiming to honor every word. Biblical scholar James Sanders argues that canon and religious community have always interacted. There is a canonical pluralism within the Bible itself that should be recognized and treasured. Those who claim that God speaks through events, through other avenues of knowledge and cultures, or through nature need discernment. This discernment interacts with the Bible.

The fundamentalist answer, although inadequate for many of us intellectually, is a powerful way of coping with the earthquake of change in the world. It must surely be a source of comfort and security for many people. Were there no political consequences to this religious view, we might appreciate its service to some people and go our own way.

But there *are* political consequences. One of the most

significant political consequences has to do with a view of the United States that was shared by many Christians at its founding—a sense that God was making a new Israel, one that would receive God's special protection and blessing above all other nations in the world. This feeling of destiny and unique purpose has provided energy and vision to our nation as America has been cherished as the instrument for bringing the whole world to Christianity. Christians have dreamed of this country as a civilization based upon Christian morality that would be a light to the rest of the world.

This vision, which has undergone mutations to take into account religious liberty and a growing pluralism in the United States, has been kept quite intact by fundamentalists. It is a covenantal relationship with God, however, and fundamentalists charge that Americans are not keeping their side of the covenant. American morality has become so degraded, according to Jerry Falwell in *Listen America*, that "If God does not judge America soon, he will have to apologize to Sodom and Gomorrah." Here is the basis for much psychic energy for fundamentalism in politics: Unless we repent and turn from our evil ways, we will lose our special covenant with God and reap judgment instead of blessing.

Christians throughout two hundred years of the American experiment have had difficulty with the concept of a Christian America as the embodiment of a new Israel. What constitutes a Christian way of life has split the Christian community, as slavery, Sabbath observance, and temperance early demonstrated. Waves of immigration into this country contributed to diversity of religious views, the growth of cities and the problems of poverty, cultural ghettoes, disparity of wealth and resources, labor unrest, and poor health. Christians have differed over whether and how to address these problems. The dream of Protestant evangelicals for an American society in which their religious view and values predominated has been disappearing, and the Prohibition movement was one of its last efforts. Today there are over fifty million Roman Catholics, seventy-two million Protestants, six million Jews, four million Orthodox, possibly almost two million Muslims, half a million Hindus, and several hundred thousand Buddhists and other Asian religious groups. The concept of one vision for a Christian civilization and a single way of life called "Christian" seems more nostalgic than real.

Meanwhile, mainline Christians in the United States, especially since World War I, have become uncomfortable with the imperialism of the new Israel vision of a city set on a hill as a light to the rest of the world. They see this concept as leading to a self-serving patriotism that is dangerously naive today. It is a humanly fallible cultural assumption to put the word "America" in the place of Israel in the Scriptures. It leads to using God to bless American actions, to claiming that *our* needs for security and economic health are more important than the needs of our neighbor nations. It leads to the assumption that God loves Americans more than the British, the French, the Italians, the Africans, the Russians, the Asians. It is only too easy to turn the universal God into a tribal god. We mainline Christians believe that the whole world is subject to the judgment and compassion of God. God uses nations for divine purposes, not ours. We must be ready for new occasions to teach new duties. American churches, including fundamentalist groups, have participated unstintingly in the great world mission movement, but even that great effort has reached a new moment in history. It is one thing to bring a new message to a strange land, quite another to interact with a church already there. American mainline churches are groping their way toward a new relationship with these younger churches born of the mission movement, a relationship of mutuality and respect.

One outcome of this new relationship to younger churches in other countries is that mainline or liberal churches are attempting to understand the world from the eyes of those younger churches to see the role of the United States from the viewpoint of Christians who are *not* American. It makes these American Christians even more uncomfortable with the new Israel view of the United States. It requires a more internationally sensitive reading of world politics than in the past. This puts mainline Christians at odds with fundamentalists on many issues and becomes a significant part of the tension between them. While becoming aware of our presumption to "conquer the world" for an American version of Christian civilization, we have learned a new appreciation for some of the unique qualities of American life. Our heritage of freedom in which religious visions may flower has become even more precious as we become aware of how unusual it is in the world. But one cannot transmit that heritage by imposition. Mainline churches are examining their faith today in relation to other world faiths. They are feeling their way toward a new internationalism that is neither paternalistic toward other cultures nor totalitarian in its claims of superiority over them.

A further political consequence of fundamentalism is its tendency to reinforce individualism, an individualism that is also self-restrained. A recent study by Peter Benson and Dorothy Williams entitled *Religion on Capitol Hill, Myths and Realities*, examines the religious and political beliefs of the U. S. Congress. One important observation from that study is that liberal and conservative Congressional leaders differ not so much in amount of religion but in kind. Conservatives tend to adopt an individualism-preserving religion and liberals tend toward a community-building religion. The researchers see the "I" versus the "we" approach as being extremely basic and pivotal and to bear a relationship to one's religious heritage. Political conservatives, some of whom are fundamentalists, seek maximum freedom for the individual, therefore a very limited role for government. Liberals in politics want certain civil liberties protected but emphasize cooperation, sharing, and social leveling. The authors of this study make a thoroughly democratic plea that all voices be heard in the political arena, and that healthy tension comes about through mutual respect. They find that the rigidity and self-righteousness of the Christian fundamentalist right is destructive of the health of democracy, but that it is saying things that need to be heard in the body politic.

How should the emergence of the fundamentalist right in the political arena be viewed? I have spoken thus far largely out of my own Christian conviction, which is challenged and judged woefully inadequate by fundamentalists. One is tempted simply to trade insults, but that, I firmly believe, puts a divine judgment upon both of us.

There is a further temptation to dismiss fundamentalists. One may accuse them of a bloated patriotism that does not serve our country well throughout the world. One may also accuse them of an archaic view of the world, one that refuses to take account of what God is allowing us to learn through our own creative faculties. Or we may rail against their overemphasis on the personal morality of sex while neglecting our more collective sins against the poor, minorities, and related social groups. We may judge them for their judgmentalism, their lack of love in declaring God's love. And we may chafe at their arrogance, self-assurance, and passionate certainty that they are on the side of the angels—and we are devils. When we learn that their numbers seem to have been greatly exaggerated, especially by television preachers, we are ready to send them back to the quiet corners of ignominy to which they were shoved after the Scopes trial.

Or we may yield to another temptation—the temptation to exaggerate their power and therefore also increase our fear of them. When one does not understand, one is more likely to fear. The national media, always hungry for a newsworthy let's-you-and-them-fight story, have contributed power and leverage to the very group about whom they are paranoid. It took television journalists a long time to measure the audience claims of the television preachers against the audience-rating tools of their own industry—and then only when a Texas sociologist, William Martin, pointed out the vast discrepancy. The energy, the sense of urgency and commitment, the startling command of financial resources from conservative millionaires, and the presence of some religious right leaders in high Washington political circles are indeed impressive reminders that simply dismissing the fundamentalist is not enough.

Somehow we must avoid either dismissing or exaggerating the role of the fundamentalist in today's social and political life. Democracy itself is at stake in our ability to hold simultaneously a concern for their right to participate and a firm resistance to their style of participation that ignores or tries to eliminate the views of others. We can at least admire the deep commitment and convictions that motivate many fundamentalists to overcome their past aversion to political involvement as they try to reclaim their nation according to their paradigm of righteousness. We can acknowledge that we, too, are unsettled by the rapidity of change, that we share anxieties while analyzing both cause and solution differently. Those of us with a deep concern for minorities, the poor, the full expression of women, and the global human community jeopardized by militarism in many nations must insist, in the name of democracy, that *these* voices also be heard, even as we urge the involvement of fundamentalists in the political arena. The Moral Majority will have its short-winded runners, their leaders who make mistakes, their coalitions that unravel, especially when power is being shared, their fickle political and financial supporters, their apathy when change takes longer than they thought. Media will move to newer, fresher topics. Administrations and parties will use ardent fundamentalists when it serves their interests and set them aside when it doesn't.

In his book *An Immodest Agenda* Amitai Etzioni argues that the Moral Majority has asked the right questions but given the wrong answers. He joins them in seeing the need for individual, social, and ethical renewal along with a revitalization of the American economy. But Etzioni sees no return to authoritarian, imposed, simple answers. He urges, however, two important ethical concepts as key to the future of our country: mutuality and civility. Mutuality is the recognition that people need deep affective bonds to one another not just to exchange services but to sustain one another as wholesome human beings. Civility requires individuals to balance their quest for self-enrichment with some dedication to shared concerns, some "common goods." Fundamentalists have both encouraged our nation to take seriously mutuality and civility and have trespassed upon them in their own righteous ardor. They have called for the nation to behave in ways that will make wholesome human beings, but they have lacked mutuality in the very definition of what it is to be "wholesome." In the name of urgent concern for the nation's well-being they have pushed in individualistic ways and in uncivil stridency their own ideas of the "common good." In all honesty many of us must confess some guilt along those faultlines as we deal with the earthquake of change.

I am indebted to Donald Dayton for a final word of hope in this catalogue of political consequences and an assessment of them. He corrected my warped historical sense of the role of evangelicals and fundamentalists in relation to some important ethical issues of the past that continue their ferment in the present. It might startle some of us to realize that the abolition movement and the feminist movement that gained impetus from abolitionism had some strong leadership from evangelical and fundamentalist figures. In pre-Civil War New York two staunchly evangelical brothers, founders of the Wall Street firm of Dun and Bradstreet, Lewis and Arthur Tappan, were so deeply involved in the antislavery movement that a mob ransacked Lewis's home and burned his furniture in the street. His wife cheerfully noted that some expensive-looking items that Lewis thought too ostentatious for prayer meetings in their home had been destroyed.

Charles Finney, the revivalist, founded Oberlin College in Ohio, and Jonathan Blanchard, who became president of Wheaton College, was a key speaker at Oberlin. Oberlin made major contributions to feminism, the peace movement, the doctrine of civil disobedience, temperance, and anti-slavery as it attempted to live up to its principle that public institutions no less than private Christians must do right, however contrary to popular sentiment. Oberlin became the first coeducational college in the world, says Donald Dayton. Some of you may be far more familiar than I with the famous Oberlin-Wellington rescue case, in which a fugitive slave was rescued *from* federal authorities in Wellington, housed in hiding at an Oberlin professor's home, and spirited off to Canada. Irate officials and solid citizens urged Oberlin students to "preach the Bible and not politics." In one high moment of history four hundred Sabbath school children marched with banners to the jail where Oberlin prisoners were being detained, and the ethics professor Peck preached that "we must obey God always, and human law, social and civil, when we can." Other equally impressive tales of an evangelical biblical fervor united with public action are told in Dayton's *Discovering An Evangelical Heritage*.

I do not know what some Wheaton supporters today do with the early radical antislavery eloquence of its president Jonathan Blanchard. Perhaps his fire for making faith real in public life has helped rekindle the new enthusiasm for conservative Christian political action. But modern fundamentalists will also have to reckon with the pacifism of Dwight L. Moody, the feminism of the Grimke sisters, Theodore Weld, and Oberlin College, the battle over free seats in the church as part of the concern for the poor as waged by the Free Methodists and the Tappan brothers, and the more recent *Sojourners* magazine concern for simplicity and its criticism of consumer capitalism. That there have been alliances of vision and action in the past between groups as disparate as liberals and fundamentalists could allow us to hope for alliances in the future.

I know of no better candidate for such an alliance than a rediscovery of a holistic pluralism in which various interest groups or caucuses are respected and encouraged, but with the common good of the society as a foundational concern not to be overridden by group interests. This means siding with Etzioni in a search for mutuality and civility.

It also means combatting the growth Daniel Yankelovich noted in American culture of an ethic built around the concept of duty to oneself in glaring contrast to the traditional ethic of obligation to others. It also means daring, in a time of strident nationalism around the world, to assert the sacredness of the total human community.

When I listen to some of the rhetoric of a Jerry Falwell, a Jim Robison, or a Pat Robertson, I despair that we will ever get beyond shouting at one another.

But we have to do with a powerful religious Word, a living God, a Holy Spirit that stirs in the church, whatever tag or "ism" may describe its various parts. If we trust this to be true, we can hope that something better may disturb our dim vision for the future as we act out our public lives, better than *any* of us now ask or think.

7

WHAT LIBERALS AND FUNDAMENTALISTS HAVE IN COMMON

Tyron Lee Inbody

There may be potential similarities between fundamentalists and liberals in the future. We liberals argue that fundamentalist paradigms of morality, beauty, and reality ought to fit the real world, our world. My contention is that we are in the midst of a paradigm change in our culture, and that the impact of that change may finally be as inevitable and as devastating for us liberals as it is for the fundamentalists. We may have to get used to the idea that we are heirs of the Enlightenment. Its values, benefits, and security may be challenged in the future as deeply as we see the fundamentalists being challenged today. Liberalism is a product of the modern period, and the modern period may be giving way to a postmodern world that will change the reality of our world.

In this contemporary battle I think we liberals tend to be a bit "priggish." This snobbery is offensive, not because it is based on bad taste or ill manners but because it is based on a degree of self-deception. We say we live in a time of radical social change. Yet our opinions are sheltered. Many of us work in institutions of learning that are almost immune to the full impact of radical change. Fundamentalists feel that change and express it in ways we label offensive, dangerous, and fascist. We hope we react and will continue to react to such change with intelligence, wit, maturity, and virtue.

But I think most of us have only begun to realize how deep and long-lasting the earthquake is that we in the Northern and Western hemispheres may have to endure. We have only begun to realize the change and threat that may be coming to our liberal institutions as our world changes. We won the battle with fundamentalists of all types for control over many of our major institutions—the universities, the seminaries, the public schools, the denominational agencies, the media. But all of these institutions and the values they have taken for granted since the Enlightenment made its impact may become more pressured by a world no longer sympathetic to liberal culture and its major values and institutions. We may begin to increasingly "feel" ourselves in the same world the fundamentalist already inhabits.

At the spiritual center of liberal culture today is a preoccupation with eschatology. Its language is focused more on fate and the human prospect than on otherworldliness and cosmic catastrophe. But the sense of disruption and impending radical change is analogous to much fundamentalist intuition. I am thinking about such representative books of liberal academic culture as: Gilkey's *Society and the Sacred*, the Club of Rome's *Limit to Growth;* Heilbronner's *Inquiry into the Human Prospect;* Lasch's *Culture of Narcissism;* Cobb's *Is It Too Late?;* Warren's *Poetry and Democracy;* Heinlein's *Revolt in 2100;* Schell's *Fate of the Earth;* and Bellah's *Broken Covenant.* Each of these in its own way reflects the stress and duress the Enlightenment paradigm is under both from internal self-contradictions and external challenges from cultures beyond northern European and American centers of power.

Slowly but surely we are coming to see ourselves, as Langdon Gilkey says, as "a culture in decline." I recall my sudden awareness upon finishing Heilbronner's *Inquiry into the Human Prospect* that the threat he felt in this book is the threat to all of the liberal values and institutions he holds dearly. What he means—and where he is probably correct—is that the prospect for North American, white, liberal culture and the values and institutions we represent may be in for a rough day. And when the liberals in the church and the academy begin to feel this in their bones as well as thinking it in their heads, we could be in the same place emotionally (and, God forbid, politically) that the beleaguered fundamentalist is today. For decades the fundamentalists have felt a challenge to their prestige, power, and security.

During these recent decades and probably for the preceding two centuries we who embraced the Enlightenment felt secure (and thus certain of our correctness) because our culture and its intellectual, political, and spiritual values were respected if not desired—at least we thought—by all peoples.

But as our beloved values—political freedom, individual rights, academic inquiry, progressive reform, prosperity, unrestricted research, rational and tolerant discourse, religious freedom, subjectivity, unrestrained criticism, the autonomous self—begin to be questioned as bourgeois ideology or subordinated to other more desirable values in a changing world, a world neither of our making nor of our liking, our feeling that we have escaped or transcended the earthquake and its devastating psychological, sociological, and spiritual dislocation may change.

There are, of course, other liberals who have a different reading of the present and future prospects for liberal culture, such as Marilyn Ferguson in *The Aquarian Conspiracy* and Barbara Marx Hubbard in *The Evolutionary Journey*. But eventually we in the North and West will be standing on the same ground. And our liberal paradigm will need to shift. Indeed, we increasingly see, in the light of the Third World critiques, that the liberal and the fundamentalist share the same world, the world of bourgeois culture. Thus from the very foundations we share the same world more than we think. The squabble is essentially an intramural squabble, one finally cast in alliance not only against premodern paradigms but postmodern non-European and non-American ones as well. I am convinced that when the prestige and security of liberal institutions is threatened and when we become self-conscious about it, we may know spiritually what it feels like to be where the fundamentalist is today.

My intent is not to be preoccupied with a pessimistic note, although I acknowledge there is something strongly Protestant, even Niebuhrian, about these comments. If we are on the verge of a movement from the modern to the postmodern world, the process will probably not be swift and self-evident, and there are equally promising and optimistic possibilities as well as negative ones. My intent is to address a word "to us" instead of "to them" or "about them" in the light of insights gained from a study of fundamentalism. And that word is that we are already in the same boat. Our liberal, academic, middle-class structure of eccesiastical agencies and academic research labs and lecture rooms is facing challenges both from within and without. They know it. They feel it in their bones. We are just beginning to get wind of it.

My conclusion is that we might (not necessarily will) respond to the change in the same way fundamentalists respond, as threatened and reactionary, the more clearly we see how radically the paradigm that liberals and fundamentalists share is being challenged by alternative visions. It is possible, of course, to believe that liberal assumptions and ideals are wholly differenct from fundamentalist ones, and that all we need to do is to live up to our alternative ideals of tolerance, generosity, pluralism, and progress so that we can avoid the fundamentalist kind of reaction. But I want to caution against the danger of believing that for two reasons.

First, the more we recognize the similarity of the social location of the two sides in this intramural struggle in the West, and the more sanguine we are in recognizing the very real danger of capitulating to the same kind of response the fundamentalist has made within the context of the larger global village, the more likely we are to be able to transcend ourselves and "live up to our ideals" insofar as they are unique and noble and call for a more generous response. The more we continue to emphasize the difference between liberals and fundamentalists, and thereby refuse to recognize our similar social location, the more danger we face of responding in like manner because we have refused to acknowledge the dynamics of our social location. One reason for acknowledging that we are sinners, that we need repentance and forgiveness, is that in so doing we are more likely to see ourselves as we are, to be able to transcend our situation, and so "to live up to our ideals."

A second reason for developing my theme is to acknowledge that self-deception is one of the most serious problems of modern culture. Our liberal assumption and assurance that we can and will live up to our ideals if we try hard enough betrays how deep self-delusion is within liberal culture. The false pride that flows from our anxiety requires more than our effort to live up to our ideals, however unique and noble they are. It requires grace—the power that judges us and empowers us to die to our insecurity and self-delusions and to rise to a new life of freedom. Our pretension to self-righteousness can be addressed to some degree by our effort to understand our situation and to live up to our ideals. But if it is not addressed also by the kind of caution it has been my task to promote, we will not draw on the full resources of grace necessary to move from this age to the next.

The self-certainty and assumed superiority of modern liberal culture and its consequences concern me as much as our hope that the fundamentalist will become as "openminded" and as "understanding" as we are. The things that have been said about fundamentalism in this book are insightful and helpful. But to set the issue as "we" versus "they" betrays a lack of understanding of the present world-situation. It precludes the grace of judgment and resurrection that liberal culture also needs in our current situation. When we look at fundamentalism today in the light of its social location, we are looking at ourselves.

8

FUNDAMENTALISM
AS A CASE OF ARRESTED DEVELOPMENT

Robert W. Shinn

If religious belief and life involve periods of growth, then a theory of human development needs to be applied in which stages can be examined and characteristics studied. Human growth is a process of expanding consciousness, valuing, and interactions in community.

Dr. James Fowler in his *Stages of Faith: The Psychology of Human Development and the Quest for Meaning,* published in 1981, describes religious development. Fowler, an ordained Methodist minister, did graduate research under Lawrence Kohlberg of Harvard University. He is also indebted to the theories and insights of Piaget and Erikson. He deals theologically with six stages a person can go through in his lifetime.

According to Fowler, faith is an innate primal response to and trust in ultimate reality. All of us grow morally, socially, and educationally in different ways and at different rates. Can it be that the religious dimension is exempt from this growth process? Fowler suggests that faith goes through several stages. After the infancy level of existence, he isolates six of these stages:

1. Intuitive-projective—ages 4-8 (early childhood)
2. Mythic-literal—ages 7 or 8, 11 or 12 (school years)
3. Synthetic-conventional—ages 11 onwards, sometimes for a lifetime
4. Individuative-reflective—ages 17 or 18, 30s and 40s
5. Paradoxical-consolidative—midlife and beyond
6. Universalizing faith—occasionally with maturity

He then defines each of these stages as follows:

1. Intuitive-projective—Rise of imagination; formation of images of the numinous and an ultimate environment
2. Mythic-literal—The rise of narrative and the forming of stories of faith

3. Synthetic-conventional—The forming of identity and the shaping of personal faith
4. Individuative-reflective—Reflective construction of an ideology; formation of a vocational dream.
5. Conjunctive (another term Fowler uses for paradoxical-consolidative)—Paradox, depth, recognition of mystery, and responsibility for the world
6. Universalist—A state reached by rare individuals who identify with humanity with exceptional sensitivity

Fundamentalism manifests characteristics of stage 3. In a more enlightened form or phase, commonly called evangelicalism, it manifests a few of the characteristics of stage 4. Characteristics from different stages can coexist in any stage. Sometimes people are caught in a very prolonged transition between stages, thereby defying classification.

From an American historian's point of view the nature and characteristics of fundamentalism can be said to have originated in the militantly conservative Protestant protest movements that crested in the 1920s, were interrupted by the Great Depression and World War II, and are now expansively enlarged in our day in divergent ways affecting the entire national scene. The contemporary expression of militant conservativism in religion, including its impact upon politics, has rightly concerned a great number of people.

From 1947 to the present the reassertion of the historic term "evangelical" (traceable to the Reformation and then the Wesleyan movement) carries its own kind of associations and ambiguities. Today it has become a canopy term for the following types of conservative Protestantism:

(1) Reformed Calvinism (exemplified by Calvin College and Westminster Theological Seminary, respectively)
(2) Revivalism-Pietism (unreconstructed fundamentalism from the earlier part of the century)
(3) Progressive evangelicalism (all the social action emphases of those who stress evangelicalism's involvement in social redemption activities)
(4) Charismatics (all those independent or denominational leaders and groups stressing their formulation of the doctrine of the Holy Spirit and the role of spiritual gifts)

According to Fowler, it is in stage 3 that adolescents reach out to "find themselves" and interpret their lives through others in the community, such as those in their peer group, school, or vocation. Childhood images of God may deepen through some experience or a distinct "conversion." Children may find the God who knows and accepts them. As the adolescent participates in society, his fervent religiosity finds expression in a system of beliefs and values from a church, synagogue, youth organization, or Bible Club.

This is the stage at which foundations can be laid for continued growth. The traditions of believing groups can become real, and individuals can think for themselves. They acquire a thought-out, tentative pattern of beliefs, potential for stage 4.

It is in stage 3 where the tyranny of "*They* say" can be most demanding and when an authoritarian religious group can exercise the greatest influence.

There are both youths and adults who are satisfied with a system that answers most or all of their questions and provides the satisfaction of an "in-group" that screens all "reality" for them. Association with a group can be a good experience. The strength orthodoxy provides is a cohesive force in any group.

But when their outlook is limited in this way, the scope for tolerance and fellowship may be narrowed. Then the forces of parochialism and fanaticism become evident to both those inside the group who are struggling to grow and those outside who have a broader understanding of Christian belief. With stage 4 people shift from relying on conventional authorities to taking personal responsibility for their commitments, lifestyle, beliefs, and attitudes. The position taken will still appear "conservative," but it is clearly an advance beyond stage 3. Their awareness of paradoxes means at least an attempt to face issues as never before. College professors in Christian higher education have an opportunity to assist adolescents in their transition to stage 4 and expose them to the higher insights and characteristics of stage 5.

Religious people often place their trust in famous pastors, TV preachers, conference speakers, evangelists, or religious authors who have a "following." This forms the pattern of conformity so typical to stage 3. When a local pastor is adored or a famous "Christian athlete" is idolized, the stage is set for a serious personal trauma when he or she "fails" them. Obvious-ly, idolization of the local pastor can affect young and old. Stage 3 is the plateau on which most people live out their lives.

The issue of role models is greatly accentuated in certain vigorous separatist or independent groups and in the kind of charismatic leadership that "shepherds." Such pastors or elders interpret Bible passages in an authoritarian fashion and pass judgment on people's personal lives to the extent of deciding who people will marry, relationships between husbands and wives or parents and children, vocational choices, and property ownership. Chapter 22 of Fowler's *Stages of Faith* consists of a 48-page case history of a young woman who was subject to such pressures, yet with difficulty survived to grow toward stage 4. Her autonomous self could then emerge and provide a foundation for authentic selfhood. Sometimes believers move from one authority figure to another in a restless search for a satisfying relationship to individuals or groups often not con-nected to mainline denominations. Fundamentalism generally thrives on dynamic leadership that requires implicit obedience.

In all conservative religious groups believers are provided with symbols hedged in with traditional interpretations to assure conformity. In stage 3 Fowler has discerned a pattern in which symbols of the sacred become inseparably connected to the sacred. In other words, for Christian groups symbols are presented as though they were identical with the realities they denote or depict. In stage 2 the Holy Bible is a very special book, God's Book, Mother's Book. Children can be in awe of it as a household fetish. In stage 3 the Bible is an authority that provides God's truth. At a naive level the Bible and all its con-tents are sacred. Therefore, you honor the Bible and God. At a more sophisticated level the Bible is the authority for conduct and belief. It is infallible or inerrant. Prophetic systems com-monly become authoritative and seen as "biblical."

Stage 2 anthropomorphic understandings of God, heaven, and hell can be carried over into stage 3 if critical discernment is not encouraged. Virginia Mollenkott in a public lecture at Eastern College reminisced somewhat bitterly about a very early period in her life when she had been indoctrinated by an ultra-conservative Protestant sect, a wing of the Plymouth Brethren. Her perception of reality was to words and expressions taken directly from the King James Bible and enforced as God's very words. Everything was screened through this verbiage, she said, and it took her years to get free of it. Stage 2 was preventing the growth of even a systematic theology characteristic of stage 3. Having wrestled with feminist theology and the study of the nature of God's attributes, she testifies to her recognition and appreciation of divine mystery in relation to the finitude of all human systems and language patterns. What a testimony to the sobering influence of a stage 5 transcendence of any and all neatly packaged systems that limit openness to all aspects of a given subject.

Stage 3 is often the time when millennial themes, prophetic views of world events, and an extreme emphasis on the Second Coming of Christ are imposed through preaching, teaching, conferences, and vividly illustrated literature. They crowd out social ethics and Christian social themes that would fulfill the basic teachings of the New Testament love ethic. Some of us are very aware of how dominant and powerful prophetic visions of the "last days" can be when you accept a system of interrelated ideas supposedly based on "rightly dividing the Word of truth." The system screens out Christian social action.

Such a system is very prevalent among vast numbers of stage 3 evangelicals and charismatics, though I do not find anyone similar to Hal Lindsey in the writings and outlook of stage 3 or 4 Reformed-Calvinist conservatives. Their amillennialism is a product of the disciplined exegesis of key biblical passages. In varying degrees they express a concern for Christian philosophy that will wholistically take into account the "natural orders" God has ordained for human community and welfare. The contrast between these two types of conservatism is quite striking and must not be overlooked.

Consider this dilemma. Stage 4 interpreters of the Bible may have to give lip service to creedal, institutional statements about infallibility or inerrancy that are officially binding upon them. Such statements of faith are often linked to seminaries, colleges, or denominations, but scholars in these institutions engage in historical-critical studies that if consistently pursued could cause them to march off the map of rigid, orthodox formulations of the nature and authority of the Bible. In very recent years we have witnessed the casuistic handling of technical distinctions between "inerrancy," "infallibility," and "verbal versus plenary inspiration." Seminary faculty members have been subjected to rabid criticism for seeking to explore the interrelations between scientific biblical studies pertaining to textual origin and composition and broad reinterpretations of biblical authority. For stage 3 conservatives such freedom of inquiry is dangerous indeed.

A stage 5 friend of mine who has been through the mill of persecution blames his experiences on blind obedience to the dogma of the Perfect Book. He looks back ruefully to a time when he himself taught Scripture and "defended the Word of God" with elaborate chicanery, artful dodges, and legerdemain. He gradually grew through stages in which inner freedom, peace, and joy were his, totally harmonious with a serious appropriation of critical biblical scholarship. He longs to join hands and heart with evangelicals of precritical understandings, but their fears of such new learning makes that impossible.

A good example of a left-wing stage 4 biblical scholar would be F. F. Bruce, retired professor and author from Manchester University. He has almost universal respect among evangelicals of various types, and he exercised his freedom to write among the rather conservative Open Brethren of the Plymouth Brethren sect in England. His studies of the various parts of the Bible, especially the life and writings of Paul and the textual nature of the Bible have earned him widespread respect and recognition. He helps stage 3 and 4 people think concretely about the structure and the meaning of the Bible. The fact that he holds to two Isaiahs and a late date for Daniel has had little or no influence among evangelicals and has not earned him disrespect!

How intricate and variable and devious can be the dynamics of change within conformity-oriented communities of believers!

One of Fowler's most valuable contributions concerns the outlook many representatives of stages 3 and 4 exhibit toward other social and religious groups. Sometimes the alternatives are seen as rivals or opponents. This is the famous "label becomes libel" way of securing in-group loyalty. It prevents the individual believer's growth in an awareness of how complex some controversial issues are. The boundaries of fellowship can be tightly drawn by what has been expertly called "cognitive conceit." It walls in truth known and sins against truth to be known.

The simplistic devices used in stage 3 and too often in stage 4 cause the "true believer" to respond to world religions as if they were toys or idols. The range and vitality of Asiatic religions, for example, may be misrepresented, underestimated, and maligned. If you believe that God only "hears" the prayers of true Christians who utter the "name of Jesus," there can hardly be the slightest empathy for the devout piety manifested by so many followers of non-Christian religions who seek ultimate reality in their own ways.

The world religions compete with Christians at whatever stage they are. Unfortunately, in even the more broadminded writings of stage 4 scholars, non-Christian religions are described abstractly. There is no effort to cultivate an in-depth sensitivity to the riches and depths of understanding and devotion the sophisticated author-teachers of those religions present. The in-group aggressive resistance to building bridges of understanding and tolerance has been called "tribalism," a term probably most popularized by that stage 5 Baptist theologian, Harvey Cox.

With reference to the Protestant world, the National and World Councils of Churches have been subjected for many decades to intense vilification. This is typical of stage 3 conservatives but frowned upon for the most part by the more thoughtful leaders in stage 4 interdenominationalism. A judicious and fair criticism of ecclesiastical bodies and their policies is always in order lest stages 3 and 4 crystallize in mainstream denominatinal Protestantism to form more patterns of conformity.

But acidic, self-serving polemics are something else. Stage 4 can be consciously interdenominational and open to a certain range of dialogue. The twentieth-century ecumenical movement with its concern for unity cultivates the voices of denominations and their particular heritages. In no other way can monolithic, stifling uniformity be avoided. Stage 5 churchmen are eager for inclusivism and the mergers that can feasibly be brought about.

Persons at stage 3 may question the statements and actions

of believers who operate at levels 4 and 5. If levels suggest a ladder of ascent, Fowler has said he would object to the picture. But he clearly favors the sophistication and scope of outlook found at stages 5 and 6. These last two stages can be linked to the highest understandings of the theme of the kingdom of God. Those who have grown into later, more advanced (a term to be taken on faith?) stages must not become condescending toward those in earlier stages. A pastor trained to live and think on stage 5 level in seminary may face the task of coping with a congregation living in nearly all stages. Stages really can coexist in us all.

Fowler has placed us all in his debt by clarifying the life of growth. He has helped us understand why people react differently to the circumstances of life and how the expressions of faith must vary.

Fundamentalism is a pejorative term—in it is no health or healing. If more churches were centers of therapeutic growth, some traits of reactionary conservatism could be overcome and growth could be encouraged without painful or traumatic transitions.

9

FUNDAMENTALISM
AND SEXIST THEOLOGY

Alvin J. Schmidt

The well-known sociologist Max Weber recognized a close and intimate relationship between the Protestant work ethic and the spirit of capitalism. When one views sexist theology, one sees a close relationship between it and the spirit of fundamentalism.

Without citing all of the various characteristics that are operative in fundamentalism, two or three stand out. John R. W. Stott says, "The fundamentalist emphasizes so strongly the divine origin of Scripture that he tends to forget that it also had human authors who used sources, syntax, and words to convey their message. . . . " Fundamentalism, says George Marsden, fears new or modern theological thought because it sees such theology as a reflection of socio-cultural change. And James Barr shows that fundamentalism "rejects or ignores large areas of modern thought and knowledge. . . . "

While these characteristics are central to fundamentalism, it seems that ignoring or rejecting large areas of thought, knowledge, and scholarship is the pivotal center. In fact, it is really the *spirit* of fundamentalism, even the fundamentalism of non-Christian groups.

Sexist Theology and Jesus' View of Women

Fundamentalists who are proud of being followers of Jesus Christ are engaged in a superb case of irony. When one reads their formulations or resolutions that are designed to keep women from teaching, or even congregational voting, it is as though Jesus never existed. In sexist theologies one finds no references to Jesus and his numerous and unusual encounters with women. In many of his interactions, as Swidler so aptly noted a few years ago, Jesus was a feminist. He defied the sexist practices of his day.

Fundamentalists overlook the revolutionary behavior Jesus displayed in his interactions with women, in part because they interpret the past in the light of their present-day culture. The fact that Jesus talked with women in public fails to arouse any real attention among sexist theologians, who apparently think that such encounters were similar to what one finds in Western societies today. Such an understanding overlooks the fact that in Jesus' time no male would speak to a woman in public. The Hebraic oral law (now recorded in the Talmud for the most part) clearly states "It is shame for a woman to let her voice be heard among men" (Berakhoth 24a). Another oral law pronouncement in Jesus' day said, "The voice of women in public is filthy nakedness" (Kethuboth II, 448).

Jesus not only spoke to women in public, but he showed his egalitarian stance even more so by teaching women and discussing theology with them. Both of these activities were theologically and culturally unthinkable to a respectable male of that time. Luke records that Mary, for instance, was "listening to his word" (Luke 10:39). This act was a flagrant violation of the oral law, which declared, "If any man teach his daughter the law, it is as though he taught her lechery" (Sotah 21b). Again, "Let the words of the Law be burned rather than committed to women" (Sotah 3:4).

When Jesus spoke to the Samaritan women, he not only showed his love to an "outsider," as fundamentalists are known to say, but he also discussed theology with her. Clearly he ignored or flaunted the religious expectations of his day as expressed in the oral law. That law emphatically stated, "He that talks much with womankind brings evil upon himself and neglects the study of the Law and at last will inherit Gehenna" (Aboth 1:5). Jesus also told the woman who first met him after his resurrection, "Go to my brethren and say to them . . . " (John 20:17). This violated yet another theological norm, namely, "Let not the testimony of women be received because of the frivolity of her sex."

Other instances could be cited showing how Jesus treated women wholly unlike the sexist theologians of his era. Still, the spirit of fundamentalism blinds thousands (especially twentieth century sexist theologians) from seeing the liberating acts of Jesus with regard to women.

There is still another irony in this posture. Fundamentalists try their utmost not to be influenced by culture in their understanding of the Bible. Yet it is precisely their present culture that prevents them from seeing what Jesus did. Current Western culture says it is acceptable for men to talk to women in public and also to permit them to learn biblical truths in various learning situations, for example, a Bible class. Thus, the import of Christ's acts are not seen as having been unconventional. Lacking or ignoring any knowledge of the extremely low status of women in Christ's time has ironically prevented sexist theologians from seeing the full measure of Jesus' love, a commodity they so highly value.

To show that the feminist acts of Jesus run counter to the sexist theology of the Rabbinic oral law is not to portray an attitude of anti-Semitism. Rather, the Hebrews, like most of their contemporary neighbors, saw women as inferior beings. To note specific instances of how sexism operated among the Hebrews in Christ's day is no more anti-Semitic than it is anti-American to show how specific acts of Martin Luther King ran counter to racism in the United States.

Ignoring the Situation-in-Life

Not only are sexist theologians, imbued by the spirit of fundamentalism, oblivious to the socio-religious culture of Christ's time, but they also tend to ignore the fact that their favorite biblical references, the ones they use to keep women silent in the church, had a cultural situation-in-life. Biblical passages are quoted and cited as though they are timeless and universal. Exegesis is performed almost exclusively by means of a syntax and grammar that fail to recognize that it is not just the Bible that sheds light on life, but also knowledge of that ancient culture.

The fifth chapter of Ephesians is used to teach that the husband is the authoritative head of the wife, in a timeless and universal manner. Such an interpretation ignores the cultural particulars that compelled the writer of this epistle. The spirit of fundamentalism forgets or rejects the thought that there was a specific reason for the husband to be head of the household. The average woman during the Greco-Roman period married at age 13 or 14 years. She had no formal education comparable to that of the man. She had no economic skills. And she was pregnant with a high degree of frequency. Moreover, a deserted or divorced wife received little or no social respect. Thus the Ephesian letter was directed primarily to "uppity" men who could easily—and many did—desert or divorce their wives, leaving them destitute. Husbands were to provide nurture as the head, not exercise power and might.

Does the socio-economic situation common to the early Christians apply today when a woman marries at age 22 with a college degree? Today a divorced or deserted woman with a college education is certainly not financially or socially destitute. Thus socio-economic changes regarding the age of marriage, fertility rate, and education of women in the twentieth century call for an exegetical reevaluation of Ephesians 5. A literalistic interpretation of this chapter appears no more appropriate than would a literalistical insistence on prohibiting women from appearing in a church service with braided hair or jewelry, as outlined in 1 Timothy 2:9. Yet sexist theology, goaded by the spirit of fundamentalism, preaches that the modern American wife, vis-a-vis the husband, is to be in "total submission without personal sin." Similar are the words of Susan T. Foh who says: "For the Christian wife, "doing right" does involve submission to her husband." Still others link subordination or submissiveness of the wife to what some call the "order of creation."

Ignoring the situation-in-life is also evident by the way sexist theologians interpret 1 Peter 3:7, which calls woman the "weaker vessel." This reference is seen as God's affirmation of the physical superiority of the human male vis-a-vis the human female. Such an interpretation, however, is not the most probable one. Gustav Stahlin shows that in the New Testament the word "to be weak" is "hardly ever used of purely physical weakness, but frequently in the comparative sense of the whole man. . . . " If it was not physical weakness that was intended, then what kind of weakness did the writer have in mind?

In the first and second centuries women were at a greater disadvantage than they are today. High rates of pregnancy coupled with primitive or no reliable medical knowledge resulted in high female mortality rates both during pregnancy and at a time of childbirth. In some instances the female mortality rate was higher than that of the male rate because girls were not nourished on an equal basis with boys. Xenophon in the fifth century before Christ mentions this practice in his *Constitution of the Lacedaemonians*. Moreover, women commonly did the more menial tasks of daily labor. These are some of the factors that accounted for the fact that women in the ancient era had a life expectancy about five years less than their male counterparts. The woman was indeed the "weaker vessel," especially in terms of survivability at that time in human history.

But is woman still the weaker vessel today? She outlives the average man in America by almost eight years and is only pregnant two or three times in her married life. Moreover, pregnancy and childbirth rarely spell death for the modern woman in Western society.

The Prescriptive View of the Bible

Frequently by ignoring the situation-in-life of its favorite biblical passages, sexist theology reads the Bible as a prescriptive code that dictates universal social behavior. It was the prescriptive reading of given references that led Luther to condemn for all time the practice of earning interest money from loans or rents. At least one of his followers, C. F. W. Walther, in the United States perpetuated the same error as late as 1864 by decrying the practice of charging interest rates. These theologians had failed to recognize that the biblical references they saw as prescriptive were no longer applicable to an industrial economy, though they were appropriate for an agrarian social structure. They failed to recognize that an industrial economy cannot function without interest monies and that it was no longer the poor primarily who borrowed, but the entrepreneurs who needed money to expand their business ventures. In short, the so-called antiusury passages, which once were prescriptive, now had become largely descriptive of a past era.

To insist on seeing the Bible prescriptively in each and every instance, especially in ethical matters, inevitably leads to absurd cultural practices or self-deception, resulting in a "cafeterial theology" in which sexist theologians pick and choose their Bible verses. When Paul commands the Corinthians to "greet one another with a holy kiss," he was definitely prescribing a specific form of behavior that fundamentalists today find culturally absurd or embarrassing. Nor do fundamentalists find it necessary to go without money when making what they call, "evangelistic calls." Yet a prescriptive reading of Matthew 10:9 calls for such behavior.

There are numerous other instances of prescriptive passages in the Bible that fundamentalists do not take seriously. I shall cite one more example, especially since it occurs in the context from which sexist theologians draw much of their ammunition. Genesis 3:18 tells Adam that he shall have thorns and thistles growing in his crops. No sexist theologian sees it as wrong or sinful when weeds are deliberately destroyed in order to obtain a more productive crop. But when Genesis 3:16 comes up for consideration, its words, "and he shall rule over you," are final and absolute. The word "shall" precludes not only Eve from having equality, but it also subordinates all women forever! However, when it comes to destroying weeds, the word "shall' has lost it force. One is hard-pressed to find a better example of what I call cafeteria theology!

Some of the errors that resulted from reading the Bible in a prescriptive and inflexible manner have fortunately come to an end. Today sexist theologians no longer say it is sinful for a woman to seek relief from pain during childbirth. Yet in 1591 Eufame Maclayane was burned at the stake in Scotland for having hired a midwife to give her pain-relieving medicine. The theologians convicted her, a woman of high social status, of violating Genesis 3:16, which says "And in pain you *shall* bring forth children."

The prescriptive understanding of Hosea 6:1, "Come, let us return to the Lord; for he has torn, that he may heal us; he has stricken, and he will bind us up," moved theologians to denounce smallpox inoculation when it first appeared in medical practice.

It is the prescriptive reading of such references as Genesis 3:16, 1 Corinthians 14:34-35, and 1 Timothy 2:10-15, along with some other citations, that deprives women of equality inside and outside the church. The prescriptive understanding of these passages, of course, is undergirded by this spirit of fundamentalism in that the sexist theology rejects or ignores relevant areas of knowledge that show the above passages to have had a specific situation-in-life, and thus are not applicable today.

•

Most of us think that fundamentalism is a relatively recent phenomenon, and primarily American. This, however, is not true relative to the *spirit* of fundamentalism. The *spirit* of fundamentalism has an ancient history, especially with respect to sexist theology. Whether it was the Hebrew priests or rabbis before and during Christ's time, the Church fathers in the early church, Luther or Calvin of the Protestant Reformation period, or the sexist fundamentalists today, they all have one thing in common—they ignore or reject data and observations that do not fit their preconceived view of women. Socio-cultural definitions were forced upon women, creating self-fulfilling prophecies that not only made men feel superior but also led them to deceive themselves by thinking that the "inferiority" of woman was God's plan and design.

What about the future of sexist theology? I would argue that the future of sexist theology is far more precarious than it is for the spirit of fundamentalism. Sexist theology cannot survive without the spirit of fundamentalism. Thus if sexist theology for some reasons becomes divorced from the spirit of fundamentalism, it will likely cease to be a significant force. The spirit of fundamentalism, however, can and likely will survive by continuing to reject large areas of knowledge that are seen as irrelevant or destructive of its theological beliefs. In short, the spirit of fundamentalism does not need sexist theology, but sexist theology does need the spirit of fundamentalism.

10
FUNDAMENTALIST
INTERPRETATION OF BIBLICAL SYMBOLS

Adela Yarbro Collins

One aspect of fundamentalism that has intrigued me is its interpretation of biblical language about personal afterlife and the destiny of the world. On my office door is a photograph of a man carrying a sign that reads "The End of the World Is at Hand!" The sign is tucked under the man's arm as he bends to scrutinize a little sign marked "Times of the Last Buses." The word "Last" suggests that the last day and the last bus [are of the same type of reality.] But as soon as the similarity is perceived, the incongruity evokes a smile. Part of the humor of the picture lies in the suggested incongruity between the fervent proclamation of the world's end and the continuing concern for the practical matters of everyday life. This jarring raises questions. How do beliefs about the end of the world relate to perceptions about ordinary reality?

I have chosen to pose this question in terms of apocalyptic symbols and fundamentalist interpretations. I should clarify at the outset what I mean by these terms. I take fundamentalist interpretation to mean literal interpretation. Literalism is based on the assumption that the words to be interpreted refer to publicly recognizable entities. Little difficulty is felt in relating biblical language about personal afterlife and the destiny of the world to ordinary, common sense language or to the language of scientific inquiry. It is assumed that when the same words are used in different contexts, they mean the same thing. The assumption is made that all biblical passages dealing with these topics can be harmonized with one another and that they are compatible with ordinary, every-day reality.

"Apocalyptic" is a modern scholarly term for literature reaching back to the third century before Jesus. Scholars have defined a literary genre they call "apocalypse" that includes the book of Daniel and other writings similar in form and content to the Revelation of John. In this literature the writer views life in this world as a shadow of things to come. Freedom and happiness can only be achieved only by the intervention of God.

My interest here is not in the genre "apocalypse" but in "apocalyptic eschatology." Eschatology is that branch of theology that deals with the last things: death, judgment, heaven, and hell. The emphasis is often on the destiny of the individual. The term comes from the Greek word for "last" and was coined in Germany in the early nineteenth century. The first recorded use of its English equivalent is in a work by an American author that dates to 1845.

In the nineteenth century, the term was used primarily in a dogmatic sense. In the twentieth century, literary and historical perspectives have overshadowed the dogmatic. The term has been redefined to take more into account the actual content of biblical and related writings. The redefinition has involved emphasis on the ultimate destiny of the Israelite or Jewish nation and of the world in general, as well as on the destiny of the individual.

Considerable scholarly debate has been devoted to the basis of a distinction between prophetic and apocalyptic eschatology, the two basic types. The notion of a personal afterlife is virtually absent in the prophetic writings. It is clearly present in Daniel 12. Modern scholars define at least Daniel 7-12 as an apocalypse. Personal afterlife is regularly present and sometimes a major theme in the Jewish and Christian works most scholars consider to be apocalypses. But it is important to keep in mind that there is considerable continuity between the eschatologies of the prophets and of the later apocalyptic writings.

So apocalyptic symbols have to do with the ultimate destiny of human individuals, the people of God, or the world. In using the term apocalyptic symbol, I am suggesting that the biblical statements about human and cosmic destiny must be understood as partial expressions of a larger myth of the End. I mean by a myth of the End a complex of stories that express the meaning of human life and the universe in terms of an ending that is to be both catastrophe and fulfillment. The existence of such a complex of stories can be inferred from the Bible in light of noncanonical Jewish and Christian literature and certain other writings. Consider 1 Thessalonians 4:13-18 (RSV):

But we would not have you ignorant, brethren, concerning those who are asleep, that you may not grieve as
others do who have no hope. For since we believe that
Jesus died and rose again, even so, through Jesus, God will
bring with him those who have fallen asleep. For this we
declare to you by the word of the Lord, that we who are
alive, who are left until the coming of the Lord, shall not
precede those who have fallen asleep.

For the Lord himself will descend from heaven with a
cry of command, with the archangel's call, and with the
sound of the trumpet of God. And the dead in Christ will
rise first; then we who are alive, who are left, shall be
caught up together with them in the clouds to meet the
Lord in the air; and so we shall always be with the Lord.
Therefore comfort one another with these words.

The opening statement, "But we would not have you ignorant," gives the initial impression that Paul intends to impart
information. This impression needs to be qualified. It is
noteworthy that this passage occurs within the second half of
the letter, which is its advisory or encouraging section. In this
portion of the letter Paul warns, advises, and exhorts. This
observation suggests that Paul is expressing a point of view and
inviting the Thessalonians to share it.

This qualification is supported by Paul's stated purpose in
enlightening the Thessalonians: "That you may not grieve as
others do who have no hope." The implication is that Paul
writes this passage to reinforce or even instill hope in the
hearers of the letter. Information is communicated, and
cognitive claims about reality are made, but in a way that fuses
insight and emotion.

One of the notions in this passage is resurrection. It was a
notion current among some Jews and Christians in the first century of the common era. But it was not yet a fixed concept. It
did not have the same meaning for everyone, not even for all in
the same community of faith. In 1 Corinthians 15 Paul can
speak of a risen body, but it is clearly a body quite different
from the earthly one. The Gospel of Luke, however, presents
Jesus' risen body in a way much more similar to the ordinary
physical body. The same variety existed among Jews.

The encouraging aspect of the passage is prominent again

at the end: "Therefore comfort one another with these words." The comfort from Paul's point of view lies in the conviction, which carries the claim of insight, that we shall always be with the Lord. As the climax of the passage, that assurance over- shadows the miraculous details, or, perhaps better, it expresses their significance, reveals that to which they point.

The informational details of this passage are difficult to harmonize with other passages dealing with similar topics. Not only that, it is often difficult to determine what the language refers to. 1 Corinthians 15:20-28 is an example. Does this passage assume a general resurrection from the dead, or only the raising of those in Christ? Is the reign of Christ from his resurrection until the resurrection of those who belong to him, which is also the end, or between their resurrection and the end that comes later? When one makes a serious attempt to discern what Paul believed about the last things, it gradually begins to become clear that logical precision is beside the point.

1 Thessalonians 4 and 1 Corinthians 15 are symbolic statements rooted in a myth of the End. This myth comes to its fullest expression in Paul's letter to the Romans:

> I consider that the sufferings of this present time are not worth comparing with the glory that is to be revealed to us.
>
> For the creation waits with eager longing for the revealing of the sons of God; for the creation was subjected to futility, not of its own will but by the will of him who subjected it in hope; because the creation itself will be set free from its bondage to decay and obtain the glorious liberty of the children of God. We know that the whole creation has been groaning in travail together until now; and not only the creation, but we ourselves, who have the first fruits of the Spirit, groan inwardly as we wait for adop- tion as sons, the redemption of our bodies.
>
> For in this hope we were saved. Now hope that is seen is not hope. For who hopes for what he sees? But if we hope for what we do not see, we wait for it with patience (Romans 8:18-25 RSV).

In this passage we see that the inner meaning of the present is expressed by evoking myths of the Beginning and the End, showing their relationship, and locating the present in the movement from origin to fulfillment.

The narrative about the fall of Adam and Eve is evoked in verse 20: "for the creation was subjected to futility." This remark calls to mind the words of the Lord to Adam, "Cursed is the ground because of you" (Genesis 3:17). Paul interprets the curse as "bondage to decay" (Romans 8:21). He invites us to view the universe as "groaning in travail" (vs. 22). Through the metaphors of bondage and travail Paul discloses reality as deeply conditioned by change and change as a profoundly threatening process. His words raise questions about what is real and permanent and remind us of what most of us strive constantly to forget: death. We share in the decay of the universe most obviously in our changing, aging, dying bodies.

But already in his formulation of the myth of the Beginning, Paul claims that we are not creatures of decay only. God subjected creation to futility in hope. The fulfillment of that hope is expressed in symbols: glory, liberty, adoption as children of God, the redemption of our bodies. In this passage Paul does not try to define what these symbols might mean in ordinary terms. He suggests that the experience of the Spirit is a symbol of what is to come. He emphasizes that we hope for what is unseen and unknown, that we hope in patience.

There are three basic modes of the interpretation of apocalyptic symbols. These are the mythic, the critical, and the fundamentalist mode. The mythic mode shares to a greater or lesser degree the mythic consciousness or mythic perspective of the authors of biblical and related apocalyptic texts. It is rare in its pristine form today, expecially in the Western nations of the northern hemisphere. But it does survive and seems to be the dominant mode for many people.

The mythic mode is tolerant of tension, including at times what seems to the logical mind to be contradiction. In 1 Thessalonians Paul implies that believers in Christ who have died are not with Christ but will rise to be with him when he returns. In Philippians he seems to assume that he will be with Christ immediately after his own death (1:23).

The mythic mode is tolerant of multiple meanings. In this way it is similar to the poetic mode. An expressive symbol in one and the same context may have more than one legitimate meaning. These meanings may be fused in such a way that the proper meaning of the symbol can be said to be the tension among the meanings, a whole greater than the sum of its parts. An example is the beast from the sea in Revelation 13. Its meaning resides in the tension among various significances: the chaos beast, the beasts of Daniel 7, Rome, Nero, and Antichrist.

When the mythic mode is living, the cognitive claims of apocalyptic symbols are accepted. Their disclosure of the meaning of present and future is believed. The hearer expects the world to be renewed and looks forward to a personal afterlife. But the details are not important. The symbols articulate the experience of the brokenness of human life and awaken and sustain hope within that experience.

For example, a person reading, responding to and interpreting 1 Thessalonians 4:13-18 in the mythic mode would not feel embarrassed by Paul's talk about bodies being changed and about believers rising to meet the Lord in the air. The main concern would be the hopeful prospect of union with the Lord.

A hearer or reader in the mythic mode realizes that this passage is not informative language in the sense of public (logically denotative) language. The fusion of insight and emotion is recognized. As expressive language, the passage discloses truth in soft focus. We will indeed join the Lord, perhaps in this way.

The Enlightenment called the mythic mode radically into question. The other two modes can be viewed as two quite different responses to the challenge of the Enlightenment. The roots of the fundamentalist mode of interpreting apocalyptic language are in nineteenth-century England and America. While rejecting the secularity of Enlightenment thought, fundamentalists absorbed its preference for clear, logical language in which words have one precise meaning. The official fundamentalist position has been that there is no contradiction among various biblical passages. The numerous statements about human and cosmic destiny can be harmonized into a coherent doctrine of the end that correlates easily with ordinary history and geography. In attempting to rescue the informational and cognitive claims of apocalyptic language, many fundamentalists have lost sight of its depth character, its plurality of meanings, and its soft focus on truth.

The fundamentalist approach to 1 Thessalonians 4:13-18 is quite different from the mythic. Not only do fundamentalists fail to stumble over the extraordinary elements of the passage, they seize upon them and make them central in defiance, as it were, of secular skepticism. The being changed and the rising into the air are not viewed as poetic statements in which the underlying hope for unity with the Lord is expressed. They are viewed rather as informational language of the same order as that of a weather forecast. Unlike the words of a weather forecast, however, Paul's statements are taken as infallible predictions and used as the basis for the fixed concept of the rapture, which has become a major fundamentalist doctrine. Rather than focusing on reunion with the Lord, fundamentalists center their attention on the consternation of those left behind when the elect dematerialize.

Much more deeply than the fundamentalist mode, the critical mode has absorbed the Enlightenment preference for clear, logical language, what Philip Wheelright calls "steno-language." The critical mode has been shaped by the post-Enlightenment development of the science of historiography. The consistent historical critic has virtually lost the mythical dimension because of the recognition that myth and history are separate. The critic recognizes, as the fundamentalist does not, that mythical time and space cannot be coordinated with historical time and critical geography. They are two different orders. Further, the critical mode has been more interested in explanation than existential understanding and appropriation.

A person reading 1 Thessalonians 4:13-18 in the critical mode who, although critical, is still loyal to the church or at least to the tradition is acutely embarrassed by the talk about the Lord descending, the presence of angels, trumpets blowing, and especially the transformation of bodies and the rising into the air. The critical interpreter emphasizes Paul's pastoral concern and is quick to explain away or translate the mythical details into conceptual language that emphasizes the notion of union with the Lord. The critical interpreter assumes, like the fundamentalist, that Paul's language is primarily informational. But from the critical point of view he was mistaken.

Where do we go from here? It should be clear that I regard

the fundamentalist mode as an indefensible barricade against the attacks of secular thinking on religious language. The critical mode has made some valuable contributions. The fact that the word "myth" has negative connotations in our culture is due largely to the critical approach. This negative assessment of myth has a limited validity. Myths and the mythic mode sometimes have pretensions of knowledge that the soft focus of depth language cannot sustain. When myths attempt to explain rather than disclose, they become pseudoknowledge. When myths are absolutized, as sometimes happens in the fundamentalist mode, they control human beings in a way inappropriate to our nature as creatures in God's image. The critical mode can teach us that *mythos* (myth) is not *logos* (rational thought).

Something is lost, however, in the insistence on the role of detached observer in the critical mode of interpreting apocalyptic symbols. The claim to disclose something about reality can too easily be ignored when it can be explained historically. What is needed today is a concerted effort to push beyond fundamentalism and combine with historical criticism a postcritical mode that recognizes the affinities between apocalyptic symbols and the best of the poetic imagination.

11

FUNDAMENTALISM
AND THE CREATION-EVOLUTION DEBATE

John N. Moore

What is the relationship of fundamentalism to the creation-evolution debate? Science is a body of knowledge obtained by methods based upon the authority of observation. Scientists observe, directly or indirectly, aspects of the *natural* environment. They do not study the supernatural or the unnatural. (The term "natural" refers to processes that exist in the physical environment yet are directly or indirectly accessible to scientists.)

Hence scientists produce orderly classifications of their repeated observations of natural objects and events. Scientists seek to test their ideas about natural objects and events by means of controlled experiments, by trial and error testing, or by tests of logical reasonableness and internal consistency.

Then what is the involvement of scientists with such terms as creationism, evolutionism, and fundamentalism? I maintain that these terms are regularly blurred and confused in the mass media, in the utterances of scientists, and even by some spokespersons or proponents of these viewpoints.

Historically, creationism was the initial world view or mainspring from which modern science developed in the 1600s. Creationism was the basis for the explanation of everything. The rise of modern science is often dated by the work of Copernicus, an astronomer, and Vesalius, an anatomist. Prior to the work of these men medieval science had been based exclusively on the authority of one man, Aristotle, rather than upon observation and experimentation. Departure from Aristotelian science came when scholars at Oxford challenged the authority of Aristotle by showing that he had made certain mistakes about natural phenomena.

Even earlier origins of science as a discipline might be found in the culture of (a) the Greeks, with their attention to logic and rules of reason, (b) the Arabs, with their attention to algebra and geometry, and (c) the Chinese, Babylonians, and Egyptians.

But according to the thoroughly documented works of award-winning scholar-physicist Stanley L. Jaki, Alfred North Whitehead, and J. Robert Oppenheimer, modern science began when the basic Hebrew world view on creation was taken seriously by such thinkers as Roger Bacon, Robert Grosseteste, Francis Bacon, Copernicus, Galileo, Vesalius, Tycho Brahe, Carolus Linnaeus, John Ray, Robert Nuttal, Johannes Kepler, and Isaac Newton.

These early scientists believed that the universe, including the earth and life on the earth, had been created by a reasonable God. They believed that God had created an orderly universe (the uniformity of natural events was assumed). They believed they could look for the explanation of any event in terms of earlier events (cause and effect was assumed), and that objective reality existed. The natural environment was worth studying, for to do so was to investigate God's creation. They believed that such investigations were possible because human beings had been created in the image of God. Human beings could find out about natural things because they had been given dominion, as God's creation, over all things.

Continued impetus for the implementation of the basic belief that an orderly universe was contingent upon the creative acts of God was given by Robert Boyle, Michael Faraday, James Clerk-Maxwell, Gregory Mendel, and Louis Pasteur (many others could also be mentioned). It is a historic fact that these leading scientists did their scientific work within the thought forms derived from the Judeo-Christian world view. Their special method of inquiry resulted in the discovery of many useful, lawful relationships that they believed were established by God, the Law-Giver.

The great physical scientists and leading biological scientists who were the "founders" of modern science realized that they had limited abilities. They limited themselves to studies that were empirical, quantitative, mechanical, and correctable.

1. *Empirical:* Science is based upon natural events and objects that can be observed. Early scientists studied things in their natural environment and used tools and made measurements to expand their ability to observe. The empirical principle of

science was a means for defining the nature of scientific beliefs. Beliefs were not regarded as scientific unless they could be tested by scientific methods.

2. *Quantitative:* Science is based upon measurements of changes in objects in the natural environment. The founders of modern science were concerned with physical reality and restricted their investigations to the kind of reality that is measurable. They deliberately altered or moved natural objects to measure changes in those objects. Physical scientists, especially, set the style in seeking to gain quantitative measurements in terms of length, weight, volume, and density. Just because values, morals, and other spiritual aspects of human beings were intangible and immeasurable did not mean they were unreal. They were merely outside the scope of scientific investigation.

3. *Mechanical:* These scientists sought to represent the order and pattern of things they found around them. They took the view that natural phenomena can and should be studied, described, and explained by reference to matter and motion. They identified scientific laws. Science, then, was restricted to the direct and indirect study of the behaviour of natural objects and events that were involved in natural cause-and-effect series. In some cases they set up physical models of what they were studying. In other instances they were only able to prepare lists, divisions, and subdivisions.

4. *Correctable:* Under repeated examination and rexamination, errors could be detected. The same results under similar conditions could be compared time after time. Through such steps these scientists were able to arrive at certain lawful relationships of natural objects and events. No scientific concepts were regarded as final but were regarded as being open to revision, and even rejection, according to their experience.

However, after two centuries of technological accomplishments many thinkers adopted other world views. During the implementation of the concept that human beings had dominion over all things, early modern scientists became easily persuaded that they could control more and more of their natural environment. Within a few centuries God was viewed mainly as the distant Creator. He was seen as an impersonal First Cause. Deism became the pattern of explanation. And as success followed success in the development of the tools of steam energy and electricity and of the whole Industrial Revolution, the pattern of explanation became naturalistic. God was outside of a closed universe. Miracles were impossible. Also a higher criticism of the Holy Bible began in Germany. It became the foundation of the development of modern liberal theology, or "Modernism."

The founders of modern science had been taught, and believed, that all things were created by God. The young Charles Darwin, for example, accepted the traditional theistic explanation of origins. He prayed to God for support and guidance. He referred to the Bible as an "unanswerable authority."

But in his maturing years Darwin changed. His faith in God seemed to shrivel as he placed greater emphasis on natural laws and neglected God's spiritual laws. He began his studies of the natural environment with belief in the special creation of all things by the Creator. His voyage around the world on board the H. M. S. *Beagle* initiated his turning from belief in special creation. During his voyage he studied Sir Charles Lyell's two-volume work on geological changes. He studied the geological features of South America and the Galapagos Islands in the Pacific Ocean firsthand. He also read Thomas Malthus's book on food consumption and human population. Apparently he did not continue his study of the Scriptures.

All of these ideas were synthesized in Darwin's thinking in such a manner that he discarded his belief in special creative acts of God as the origin of living things. It was replaced by his own belief that competitive interactions of many variations of living things in natural environments resulted over lengths of time in changes in organisms. Some became extinct and others produced new varieties that presumably became new kinds of organisms. He called his imagined process "natural selection."

His explanation of how changes in living things supposedly came about on the earth was read by such contemporaries as the noted British philosopher Herbert Spencer. They adopted the phrases "survival of the fittest" or "struggle for existence" to express Darwin's ideas. Victorian Englishmen knew much about wars, diseases, famines, and weather conditions, so the idea of competitive struggle was easily understood. They believed Darwin had explained how living things "evolved."

Evidently Darwin's own turning from belief in special creation because he became insensitive to the Bible and the spiritual laws of God was more or less characteristic of many leading English scholars at the time. Darwin set an example for such "free thinkers." Many of the scholars attracted to Darwin's ideas had never carefully studied the book of Genesis or theological writings on the special creative acts of God regarding the origin of the heavens and the earth. Thus they were not personally armed with the Bible's unchangeable answers about ultimate origins.

Hence, most English scholars were "susceptible" and became confused by the various speculative ideas and imaginations of Darwin and his followers. They were vulnerable to so-called naturalistic, nonsupernatural ideas. Victorian Englishmen were easily persuaded that the "natural selection" of living things occurred analogously to the selection of domestic organisms, to groups of human beings with "class" status, to nations competing in world economies, and to warfare. *But Darwin never established scientifically that "natural selection" was a means whereby a presumed evolution occurred.*

Darwin published a lengthy series of persuasively presented arguments. In actual fact, no scientist has ever been able to scientifically study the origin of any new kinds of organisms. This is because scientific study entails either direct or indirect observation of repeatable events. The primary pattern that occurs is a remarkable genetic constancy of reproduction of easily recognizable plants and animals. No new kind of plant, no new kind of animal has ever been produced.

Without a doubt no other author in the nineteenth century influenced human thought around the world more than Charles Darwin when he published his two books, *The Origin of Species* and *The Descent of Man.* Darwin and his followers worked essentially to "un-God" the universe. That position was far from the outlook or viewpoint from which modern science developed.

In a word, after the Copernican displacement of the earth as the center of the universe came the Darwinian displacement of human beings as distinct creations of God. Thus human beings were seen as part of the flow of natural events, part of a supposed continuum with other animals. Human beings were no longer considered the distinct, unique creations of a personal, Creator God.

Thus fundamentalism was a 1920s movement primarily by ministers and theologians to correct spiritual and intellectual commitments in the United States. Religious fundamentalists were convinced that evolutionary thinking by scientists and Modernism in theology would destroy Christianity as an effective moral force in the nation. Opposed to "evolution" in science and liberal thinking about the Scriptures in theology, proponents of fundamentalism held forth for a restatement, a revitalization of the frame of reference, of the world view from which their traditional faith derived.

Fundamentalists supported a biblical creationism based on a literal reading of the Holy Bible. Totally unwilling to follow either the higher critics of the Bible or modern liberals in the mainline denominations, fundamentalists insisted upon "Five Points:" (1) the infallibility of the Bible, (2) the virgin birth of Jesus Christ, (3) the substitutionary atonement of Jesus Christ, (4) the bodily resurrection of Jesus Christ, and (5) the second coming of Jesus Christ. These were the clear essentials of a campaign to lay the basis for the spiritual and moral revival in the United States.

However, fundamentalists only enjoyed success against evolutionary thinking and textbooks in Oklahoma, Florida, North Carolina, Texas, Tennessee, Mississippi, Louisiana, and Arkansas. Also they made only limited inroads against increasing denominational accommodation to the nontraditional views of Modernist theologians.

Eventually fundamentalists implemented the doctrine of "separation from evil things." Thus by 1930 leaders had come and gone, and adherents of "the fundamentals" actually "withdrew" from academia to establish separate seminaries, churches, educational institutions, and even an American subculture in various Bible-belt regions of the country. The net result was isolation from academia, which has continued to a great degree to the present moment.

With the diminished intensity of the fundamentalists an intellectual vacuum came to exist. In the early decades of the twentieth century many scholars changed the four limiting principles of science into dogmas, into various forms of scientism. Scientism is a belief that only the methods of the natural sciences can be used fruitfully in the pursuit of knowledge. Whereas professional scientists properly limit themselves to study of the interrelationships of matter and energy, modern practitioners of scientism are motivated by the viewpoint that the only reality is matter and energy.

According to scientism there is only up-to-date scientific knowledge. All else is nonsense. As a consequence many scholars are proponents of empirical scientism, psychological scientism, and sociological scientism. They are devotees of empiricism, or materialism, or determinism, or utopianism as world views by which they gauge all reality.

And the broadest, most inclusive form of scientism is evolutionism. Evolutionism is the view that *all* reality resulted from the evolutionary emergence of stars, planets, comets, galaxies, and more and more complex life forms from inanimate matter to Homo sapiens. Today evolutionary thought is so broadly applied that one can speak of total evolutionism, including stellar evolution, molecular evolution, organic evolution, and cultural evolution. But many of the careful, accurate laws of modern science are violated by various proponents of total evolutionism.

Many astrophysicists violate the law of the conservation of matter and energy (matter and energy can neither be created nor destroyed) when they teach, write, and insist upon belief in an unnatural "Big Bang" origin of the universe. Many reductionist biochemists violate the law of biogenesis (life comes from previously existing life) when they teach, write, and insist upon belief in an unnatural spontaneous generation of submolecular units of matter to form life substance. Many megaevolutionists violate the laws of Mendel (the laws of segregation and recombination) when they teach, write, and insist upon an unnatural animalistic, anthropoid origin for human beings. Actually such total evolutionists can quite properly be thought of as neofundamentalists.

Yes, many astrophysicists, reductionist biochemists, and megaevolutionists are neofundamentalists. Neofundamentalists are those persons who believe: (1) there is no God, (2) matter is eternal, (3) no miraculous, supernatural events are possible, (4) life substance is the consequence of inherent propensities in eternal matter, and (5) human consciousness and bodily form derived from animal consciousness and bodily form.

However, this broadened viewpoint, which is so dominant in the 1980s and which has developed in a little over a century since Darwin, is without any significant repeatable empirical data from naturally occurring events.

Actually evolutionists speak glowingly and write ingeniously about numerous unnatural concepts, such as (a) a supposed "Big Bang" explosion of a dense substance of unknown origin, (b) spontaneous generation of living substance from nonliving matter of unknown origin, (c) mountain building due to the movement of dry rock masses, (d) the division of one land mass into existing continents, and (e) the appearance of new physical traits through presumed mutational changes. But all of these ideas are totally without any conclusive empirical support from studies of naturally occurring events of the magnitude involved in such concepts. Total evolutionists commonly do *not* deal with natural events, but with imagined unnatural events.

Yet the circumstantially grounded total evolutionary point of view is the world view that has been adopted by influential scholars in every major academic discipline of human thought. In a word, all disciplines of human thought are focused around the theme of total evolutionism as the dominant explanation of origins among intellectuals today. Evidently what Darwin wrote was just what the mainstream of academia in England and elsewhere was waiting to read.

Today total evolutionism is the supreme overriding world view adopted in all major disciplines. The full range of research in the history of ideas substantiates that selected indoctrination among the intellectuals of the world has increased ever since the publication of Charles Darwin's book *The Origin of Species* in 1859. Darwin did not invent "evolution," but his books seemed to support a world view the intelligentsia of his day wanted.

Consequently in the 1980s spokespersons for creationism are heard once again. Scientific creationism is a movement primarily by diligent scientists to correct the unnaturalistic direction of the scientific discipline. Whereas many present-day scientists believe in scientism and think in terms of highly imaginative unnatural speculation about the question of origins, in contrast, modern creationist scientists are implementing a revitalization of a fully objective scientific endeavor.

Modern creationist scientists base their position on the same presuppositions of cause and effect and the uniformity of nature as did early modern scientists. Thus modern creationist scientists are working to restate the historical "roots" of early modern science before scientism became dominant. Modern creationist scientists are working to show that proper, orderly scientific work is accomplished only within the parameters of truly empirical, quantitative, mechanical, and correctable scientific studies.

Therefore scientific creationism is a scientifically based viewpoint. It is essentially a mainspring for the 1980s. All carefully derived, objectively substantiated scientific data of the physical and biological sciences can be used to support belief in the Designer, Creator God as the creator of all things. An implementation of the viewpoint of scientific creationism would correct:

1. the present monopolistic, exclusive teaching of total evolutionism based upon the Darwinian reactionary, substitutional world view presently adopted in place of the Judeo-Christian theistic philosophical ground of the modern scientific discipline;

2. the steady equivocation of the term "evolution," whereby distinctions are ignored between (a) documented limited genetic variations within easily recognized plant and animal forms and (b) a fully imaginary, grand-scale gradual change of life substance from single-celled forms to more and more complex forms;

3. an unquestioning predisposition by grand-scale evolutionists regarding a supposed animalistic, anthropoid origin for human beings (even the presumed origin of the human brain from a reptilian brain), contrary to all information about the uniqueness and distinctness of human beings genetically and in symbolic conceptualizations;

4. the unqualified practice of extensive extrapolation from data about limited changes of complex organisms gained from present human experiences to supposed, imagined, speculated changes of constructions of past plant and animal life presumed

to have existed on the earth; and

5. the identification of *estimates* of time with regard to past objects and events with regard to the conceptualizations of all persons thinking about "ages" before historical time when records of human activities are available. Modern scientists are able to formulate only estimates of time in the prehistoric past. Scientists do not measure past eons of time, since no calibrated geochronometer exists.

Scientific creationism is an effort by *scientists* to restate, to revitalize the historical base of early modern science before scientism became dominant. American Civil Liberties Union proponents cannot prevent the teaching of young minds that the modern scientific discipline is rooted in the Judeo-Christian world view. ACLU leaders cannot ignore the fact that proper, orderly scientific endeavor involves four limiting principles and that fully scientific studies of natural objects and events are empirical, quantitative, mechanical, and correctable.

Further, ACLU leaders and their scientific peers cannot ignore the order, regularity, and pattern of stars, planets, comets, galaxies, cellular life, the exclusively "left-handed" protein structure of every living thing, complex organelle and organ interactions, human language complexity, and the genetic reproductive constancy of easily recognizable plant and animal forms. Such order, regularity, and pattern constitute excellent present-day, repeatedly observable, circumstantial evidence for belief in a Designer, Creator God.

Scientific creationism is a mid-1980s correction effort by diligent scientists to redirect the attention of their scientific peers to the study of natural objects and events, in contrast to stress upon such metaphysical "will-o'-the wisps" as the "Big Bang" explosion, the spontaneous generation of living substance, and the animal origin of unique, sentient human beings. The pursuit of such metaphysical substitutes for reality are fully outside of proper, orderly scientific endeavor.

12
CREATIONISM
AS A REJECTION OF RESPONSIBILITY

Michael H. Barnes

Creationists reject the theory of evolution—not merely the neo-Darwinist theory of how evolution took place, but even the more basic idea that present life forms are all biological descendents of an earliest simple life form. In doing this, creationists are not merely rejecting a particular scientific theory, they are also rejecting a whole style of thought that humankind has been developing and practicing to its benefit for the last three or four hundred years, a style of assuming responsibility for our lives.

Since the time of Galileo people have become more and more accustomed to operating on the double supposition that events have natural explanations and that it is our peculiar talent and responsibility as persons to do our best to discover those explanations. It is this supposition that has led to the elimination of smallpox and the creation of new agricultural methods. It has also promoted free inquiry as well as the free speech and democracy that support it. It has prompted people to take more responsibility for the conditions of their lives, including the moral, social, political, and economic conditions. It is *the* supposition on which modern science is based.

In a sense science is quite simple. It is a process of paying attention to the facts, of devising various explanations as to why the facts are as they seem to be, and then testing both the fact-claims and the various explanations in *all* relevant ways available.

The overall test of fact-claims and explanations is whether things *fit* together. Do the facts, as they appear, really fit with other facts? Do the explanations fit the facts, and do they fit with other explanations? Science supposes, as we all suppose in our daily lives, that when our ideas fit with each other they are more probably correct. When they conflict, then one or more is probably incorrect. The more all the facts and explanations fit together in a vast interconnection, the more reasonable it is to suppose they are correct. This simple process of science, however, turns out to be quite complex in actual practice. And the complexity provides many an opening for creationists to insert various objections.

All the supposed facts we perceive are in some degree interpretations made by our senses or our instruments. The sun does not really rise in the East, a smooth tabletop is in fact a rugged surface formed by electromagnetic fields, and viruses may or may not deserve to be called living. Separating what is just "there" and what is our way of understanding what is there is always only partially successful. The patterns we see are themselves also interpretations to some degree. Whether they are the correct or most appropriate interpretations can be determined only by continuing to apply the same criterion of fit: do these patterns we see fit with all other relevant facts and patterns of facts?

It would seem that creationists are concerned with facts, especially in their arguments with evolutionists. Some creationists' texts are extraordinarily full of detailed analyses of pieces of evolutionary evidences and ideas. But creationists tend to be highly selective in their use of facts, careless of the overall "fit" of facts with *all* other relevant facts. They select some specific anomalies about beetles or geological layers or radioactive decay in order to throw an objection into the pot. They are interested in looking at some parts of the fact-claims biologists make about anthropods, or geologists make about the earth's crusts, or physicists make about the formation of elements in the lifespan of suns.

But among the great amount of creationist literature there is no *overall* description of the patterns of facts in geology or genetics or comparative anatomy and population distributions. There is no real test, either, of how all the ideas from these fields really fit together.

The obvious reason for this is the confidence that creationists have in their alternative general account of how the various life forms appeared on this planet. If they are sure they already have the correct pattern of facts from revelation, there is little need to spend years collecting and organizing information. They have a shortcut to truth.

But there is something more serious going on in the creationist's approach than just a nonscientific approach to learning the facts. This is partly clear in that creationists accept the scientific criterion of whether the facts fit together. When creationists leap gleefully on any of the anomalies about beetles or whales or earthfolds, they reconize the power of the criterion of fit. They know that if there is some factual instance that does not fit with the supposed pattern—the pattern evolutionists perceive, in this case—then that pattern might not really be there. It might be a mistaken interpretation. Creationists are caught in a strange position on this point. They recognize the validity of the criterion of fit, but they do not apply it fully and consistently.

In addition to the matter of facts and their patterns (and the varying degrees of interpretation that are part of them), there is a second major aspect to science, the formulation of explanations for the facts and their patterns. This is the realm of theory. Most theories are hypotheses about what is not directly visible. The theory of gravity, for example, is about an invisible force that explains some of the behavior of physical bodies. The theory of atoms is about invisible clusters of invisible particles that account for various chemical and other events. These invisible realities may or may not really be there. They are products of our imagination in the sense that we never see them. We only can say that it is very reasonable to believe they they—or something very much like them—are really there in order to account for the facts we can see.

Because these invisibles are products of our imagination in some sense, we can never be fully sure they are the truth. Instead we have to remember to treat them as theoretical realities, even if they are the best hypothetical realities we have been able to imagine so far.

To determine which of these hypothetical realities is best as an explanation for certain events or patterns, we have to test how well the theories fit the facts. We again look for overall logical coherence, for fit. When a theory fits well with the facts, it is a plausible account of the facts. When a theory is the only one available to fit with the facts, it becomes reasonable to use it as the best available theory. When the theory fits also with other facts and other theories that work well, then the theory becomes even more plausible. The long term goal behind any theorizing is to produce theories that fit so well with so many other good working theories, as well as with all relevant and available facts, that this overall coherence of all our ideas and facts becomes the major argument in favor of the correctness of the theory.

The theory of evolution is precisely such a case. The geological evidence is best explained by a theory that says there have been continuous forces at work for billions of years. There is no alternative competing theory that actually deals with *all* the evidence contained even in a basic textbook in geology. God might have created the world to look as though it evolved geologically, but this makes all the appearances deceiving.

Likewise the evidence from comparative anatomy long ago presented the possibliity that all living species were related in some way, as though members of a family tree. God might have made things that way, as creationists almost argue. But their theory on this single point at least does not outweigh the evolutionist one.

Genetics is another area that has its own theories. Mendel postulated the existence of invisible genes that determined the characteristics of offspring. In time his basic idea proved rather accurate. Moreover, this also turned out to be compatible with the theory of evolution. In our own time, knowledge of DNA, genetic structures, and various protein forms constitutes a set of theories that are supported by excellent evidence. In addition, these theories fit quite well with the basic notion that evolution has taken place. Again, God might have done all this by divine decree for inscrutable purposes. But this would once more make appearances deceiving.

On the whole, the hypothesis that life today is the result of an ongoing evolutionary process, probably from a single original life form, is a theory that embraces many other theories and fact-claims in a network of interlocking coherent logic. The basic theory that evolution took place is so well consistent with all that we know from many fields that to seriously doubt it has become unreasonable.

In the face of this it is almost startling that creationism has survived with such strength for so long. Confidence in the Bible is again a partial reason. There must, however, be further reasons why the creationist *interpretation* of the Bible has prevailed among many Christians in spite of the availability of alternative interpretations more compatible with the best available understanding of facts, patterns, and theories tested rather thoroughly by the criterion of overall fit. (Creationists, for example, are quite willing to interpret the notion of "firmament" in the first chapter of Genesis in a modern way, rather than continue to think of the sky above as a hard shell. Yet most will not interpret the word "day" in a way that will allow for millions or billions of years of a developmental evolutionary creation "day" by "day.")

One basic reason, of course, is loyalty to family and tradition. Our beliefs, values, identity, and sense of belonging are all tied together in each of us, and no part of the weave is easily unthreaded without weakening the whole, something each of us would prefer to avoid. In many cases it may also be a defensive sectarian consciousness at work, in which creationism is a badge of faith that identifies the true believer and separates her or him from the corrupt outsider. To some extent creationism is also a lingering effect of an ignorance about the theories of evolution, what they do and do not claim, and what the evidence is for and against them. Unfortunately, evolutionary theory has not been treated that thoroughly in many high school biology classes, so it is not surprising that many people are misinformed about it.

To some extent also, creationists are simply naive in their general understanding of science, not so much directly opposing it as failing to see how it actually operates. Creationists have insisted that evolution is not a fact (nor a pattern of facts?) but a theory—a hypothesis formed by human imagination—rather than fact. Therefore, they say, evolution should not be treated as a fact. Perhaps so, but on those grounds neither should gravity and atoms be treated as facts. Similarly, creationists insist that science is only that which is laboratory-tested under controlled conditions. While it is true that controlled laboratory manipulation of variables is an excellent way to test theories when possible, that is by no means the only way. A theory is tested by its overall fit with any relevant facts, patterns, and other well-tested theories. Ideally, there are fact-tests that could show a theory to be false, but many of these are not laboratory controlled tests. Often the best that can be done is to keep looking for such falsifying data wherever they might show up. Astronomers look to the skies, geologists look to the earth, and evolutionists look to information from fossils and population distribution—all of this outside of the laboratory in rather uncontrolled conditions.

Once again, creationists recognize this when they use information taken from uncontrolled nature rather than from the laboratory to attack the theories of evolution. They consider the challenges they raise concerning the development and function of the eye or the probabilities of amino acid formations in nature to be valid challenges, even though they are often based on a theory that is not always testable in the laboratory. But they do this in the same partial or odd way they use the criterion of fit in regard to facts and patterns. They refrain from constructing an all-embracing theory to make, say, biblical data and evolutionary evidence and theory fit together in any sort of grand synthesis. (Teilhard de Chardin and Alfred North Whitehead have both shown that something like this can be attempted.)

Among creationists there are individuals with advanced technical or scientific degrees, such as John Moore and Duane Gish, who might attempt such a synthesis. The necessary imagination and ingenuity and desire to make overall sense of things is demonstrated by dispensationalists and apocalypticists and creationists alike. Yet it still lacks. Creationism has not produced a theory of life and creation that has an overall fit with both a respectable and reverent interpretation of the Bible and also with all the data, patterns, and theory relevant to the idea of evolution.

The answer to this, I believe, is that creationists do not grasp the full implications of what science is and how it operates. This is not just an intellectual failure. It is also a particular lack of the faith and values that support the modern scientific enterprise.

There are two aspects to the basic faith behind science. One is the faith that reality possesses a (God-given) inbuilt coherence and intelligibility. That faith is expressed every time a person applies the criterion of fit, expecting that things must coherently fit together. It is a highly reasonable faith. The success of science is evidence for that claim. But it is never fully provable, so an element of faith (belief/commitment) is involved.

The other aspect is the faith that we humans possess an intelligence (God-given) that can grasp the intelligibility of reality through *our* theories and *our* interpretations of the facts and their patterns. This second aspect of faith is an affirmation of the fundamental legitimacy and worth of being what we seem to be when we do science. We are active knowers interpreting the world out of belief and interest in its intelligibility and out of a faith in the legitimacy and worth of ourselves as knowers.

To a creationist it may seem we have two fundamental options here. One is to submit ourselves to the true word of God found in the Bible. Such submission can use aspects of science to reject science when it threatens what is supposedly the literal word of God without thereby becoming fully scientific. So the creationist can use the criterion of fit to challenge the theory of evolution, even while never submitting his or her own beliefs completely to that criterion. To do so would be an acceptance of the other option, which is to have faith that we and the world are constituted (by God) in such a way that using the scientific method thoroughly is legitimate and worthwhile.

This second option places great responsibility on us. We ourselves would have to carry the burden of determing what is true and what is not. We would have to use the criterion of fit to judge all the various interpretations of reality that are the theories, patterns, and facts that science uses. An implication potentially dangerous to some religious belief exists here. Can and should we apply the criterion of fit to all truth-claims, even traditional religious ones, thereby assuming responsibility for our religious interpretations of the world or our interpretations of the Bible? Consistently enough, the creationists reject this in their claims of the literal inerrancy of the Bible, as though our understanding of the Bible (as well as the understandings of the writers?) were not also *interpretations* to some degree. Creationists would insist that we just need to read, accept, pray, and obey.

In the end, full-scale scientific thought may be unacceptable to creationists, not merely because in some instances it would undercut the internal plausibility of some scriptural statements, but because full-scale scientific thought represents a basic attitude—or faith—that is unacceptable to creationists. The full scientific approach is an act of self-confidence and self-determination, inasmuch as it represents a willingness to make the investigator the one who determines through observation and interpretation and testing what is true and what is not, and inasmuch as it has faith in human abilities to rightly make such determinations. A number of studies have indicated that for many people their religiousness is associated not with such self-confidence and freedom but rather with a sense of relative lack of power and with a low self-acceptance. There are other possible explanations. James Fowler's analysis in his book *Stages of Faith* includes some relevant observations about the intellectual style of different kinds of religiousness.

Whatever the reasons, creationism is a rejection not only of the scientific method but also of the faith and values that underlie it. That faith and those values are not guaranteed to be justified. To trust in our own human intelligence as the source of truth and as a legitimate tool for reinterpreting even some traditional religious beliefs is a somewhat bold act of faith. We humans are notoriously subject to self-deception, ignorance, stupidity, and sheer wrong-headedness. Yet the creationists pay a terribly high price when they reject science in favor of submission to their interpretation of biblical statements. If we sacrifice faith in our ability to interpret reality through the use of reason, as in science, we also sacrifice some of our responsibility for doing the best we can with what we have. Science has turned out to be very effectively important in curing disease and feeding millions. The scientific approach is still an effective corrective to prejudice and foolishness based on ignorance.

Most importantly, if we sacrifice faith in ourselves as capable knowers, we sacrifice part of our selfhood. To be able to learn facts, recognize patterns, imaginatively construct theories and demand logical coherence of them, and evaluate reflectively the validity of our theories and fact-claims is a major dimension of what is it to be human rather than just another animal. Religious faith need not be intellectual. There are various ways of relating to God, to the ultimate source and goal of existence. But a style of religious thought that stands against a thorough use of our capacity for honest and self-critical reflective understanding is one that sacrifices a core part of our humanness. Unwittingly, it seems, this is what creationism does.